SRI SITARAMAYANA

AN EPIC IN POETRY

Veda Samhita

This book is dedicated to

The two people

I love and respect

More than God,

My parents,

Dr. R. S. Madhavi and R. Rajeev Chandra

And

My Younger Brother

R. Advith Hruday

ACKNOWLEDGEMENTS

Though it is me who has written this rather long poem, I received tremendous help from a lot of wonderful people. I first and foremost thank my grandfather and my literature guru, Sri R. Seeta Rama Rao for inspiring me to write Sri SitaRamayana. I also must thank him and my beloved father Sri R. Rajeev Chandra for patiently listening to every single line of this poem. I extend my gratitude to my maternal grandfather Sri T. R. K. Janardan for typing the entire poem that I had written on paper and digitalizing it. I also want to show my gratitude to my grandmothers Smt. R. Sarada and Smt. T. Dakshayani for telling me tales from not only Ramayana but many other Hindu Gods as well. I must thank my Mother Dr. R. S. Madhavi for supporting me in whatever decisions I make and making sure that I had enough discipline to complete those decisions. I also must thank my proofreader, my younger brother R. Advith Hruday for reading through my book. I also thank my cousin K. Abhishek for picking up my calls even past midnight and patiently clearing all the doubts that I had in Ramayana. I also thank my best friends Dhyuthi Taman, Sri Padma, Anuhya Arun, M. Sri Navya and M. Sri Nitya and my cousin sisters Lasya and Thrilokya for listening to my hour long ramblings about this poem. I also thank my cousins Vinuthna, Amogh, Ananya Medha and Vibhav for listening to my tales. I should also thank my baby cousin Abhirav, who even though cannot read yet, will hopefully be one of the first kids to grow up reading my book. I also thank my uncles and aunts Dr. K. P. Srinivas Rao, Smt. Deepa; Sri R. Rakesh Chandra, Smt. Sneha Latha; Sri T. Ravi Shankar, Smt. Kiranmai;

Sri T. Shiva and Dr. T. L. Sravanthi for their ongoing moral support. I also would like to thank, with all my heart, my English teacher, Ms. Dipti for acknowledging my poetry and advising me to pursue it. I would also like to thank my pet dog Frizbee for always cheering me up. Last but never the least, I whole heartedly thank you, for reading the first book I ever wrote.

With Love

Veda Samhita

FOREWORD

सीतायाः चरितम् महत्

("Sitayaah Charitam Mahat") is what Sri SitaRamayana is about.

Veda Samhita authored it very sincerely under the able guidance of Sri Ravulapati SeetaRama Rao Garu, her paternal grand-father, himself an eminent writer and an acclaimed officer of unflinching principles.

Veda's poetic narration of the great epic has the speed of a steadily flowing river and the fragrance of ardent devotion to detail. Its vocabulary is simple, narration is straight-forward and rhythm is easy to catch.

Taking up this huge task as her very first project while she is still in her early teens and completing within two years speaks high of her devotion and determination.

May the principles imbibed in this great epic inspire her and her readers into a life of exemplary principles and enlightened living.

T. R. K. Janardan

Sitting below the mango tree

I turn the first page of this book

The story of Sita and Rama do I see

This epic Ramayana gets me in a hook

This beautiful story I read and read

And read this book throughout

In my mind it plants a tiny seed

And into a tree of wisdom does it sprout

This story revolves around a person

Sri Rama is that person's name

He is said to belong to the clan of Sun

In him, he has no mistakes to blame

Once Valmiki was sitting under a tree

And sage Narada came to his village

Valmiki said "O' Sage, thank you for visiting me

For I have a doubt that can only be cleared by a sage

O' Sage, please answer my question

Is there a man as bright as the Sun?

Who looks like the Moon's mighty reflection?

And of his kind, he is the only one?

~

He knows and goes in the right way

The whole world, his brightness could stun

The more you praise, there is more to say

Tell me, O' Lord, is there such a son

~

Bless me, O' Sage, by giving me his name

Name that man who is the gem amongst the treasure

Name him, who is simple, yet having fame

Name him who does not get angry even in pressure"

~

Upon this question did the sage smile

He replied "Your question has pleased me,

I have walked around the world, mile by mile

Yet in only one man this greatness I see

~

Rama is the greatest man I have ever seen

Amongst the darkness, he shines like the sun

He walks in the path rightful and clean

In this world he is second to none

Knowledge of Ramayana to you I shall present

For whoever shall hear this tale

And know whatever the story has meant

To be happy forever, they shall never fail"

After listening to him, Valmiki was pleased

In this world such a man is truly there

Finally Valmiki's doubt was eased

Of Sri Rama, Valmiki was finally aware

Valmiki then went to the stream,

To cleanse himself and pray

He saw there, two birds, loving like a dream

On a beautiful branch they both lay

For a moment the sage was still
In those birds' beauty, he went adrift
Abruptly one of them, did a hunter kill
He killed it, with an arrow swift

The hunter's actions angered the sage
From Valmiki, a few words came
Those words formed a curse of rage
That curse seemed to be set aflame

While going back, he found it strange,
A poem is what his words formed
In him he felt a sudden change
He felt like he was transformed

He prayed to God by closing his eyes
In him, Lord Brahma he could see
The Lord told him that he had a prize
And that the poet in him is free

Then did the sage decide to write,

To write a book about that man

In Rama he could feel knowledge bright

Then to write Ramayana did the sage plan

Ramayana he wrote with love and devotion

In Ramayana, he poured his heart out

Ramayana is a mixture of many an emotion

It is a story with perfection throughout

Sarayu was a great river,

On its banks was Kosala built

Its king Dasharatha, was a well-known giver

His subjects were loyal and thus had no guilt

Ayodhya was the capital of the land

It was a majestic city of hues bright

By the greatest architect was the city planned

Such that every corner would have light

Ayodhya was ruled by the clan of Sun

Dasharatha was its supreme king

And his people had troubles none

Every corner bloomed like the season spring

As his queens, three women the king had

Kausalya, Sumitra and Kaikeyi were they

But whatever they did, they did not have a lad

And the solution to this problem, no one could say

Once, in the court, the king was there

He was advised by one of his subjects true

To conduct Ashwamedha yagna to have a heir

This was the only way to end the king's blue

Ashwamedha yagna so did he conduct,

So did he conduct with pomp and show

The greatest of priests were present to instruct,

And many pundits told him all he wanted to know.

He donated to people, one and all

He donated to people, regal and grand

He donated to people, mighty and small

He donated to people, from all over the land

The king prayed to the Lord, to have a child

Putrakameshti yagna he conducted after this

The Lord soon gave some custard and smiled

The offered custard the king accepted with bliss

The custard, between his wives, divided the king,

Within a year, with sons, he was blessed

So much happiness to Dasharatha did it bring

That moment, in his life was the very best

Rama was queen Kausalya's one

Lakshmana and Shatrughna Sumitra bore

And Bharata was Kaikeyi's son

And all the four kids did the king adore

All the four grew up to be great

All the four were the very best

All the four, no one could hate

Everywhere they went, it felt like a fest

The four grew up to be handsome and tall

The four were witty and kind

The four were admired by one and all

Brothers better than them one couldn't find

King Dasharatha was in the court one day

He was discussing about the princes' wedding

Just then a visit did sage Vishwamitra pay

To welcome him came himself the king

With a rain of flowers did the king greet

The sage was treated by the king with utmost care

Him with devotion did the king treat

For Vishwamitra, he made a heaven there

Then he said, "O' Great sage, welcome to my place
O' Great sage, ask for anything you seek
Ask for anything in this entire space
Your wish shall be fulfilled as soon as you speak

Ask for anything strong or weak
Ask for anything made of stone or gold
Ask for anything common or unique
Ask for anything new or old"

A smile showed that the sage was pleased
"You spoke like the true heir of Sun
I have problem that should be eased
And for it to be eased I need your son

There is a yagna I need to complete
But some deadly demons are stopping it
Those demons only Sri Rama can defeat
So to take him with me, please permit"

To this wish the king was shocked
Into such a peril, his son, how could he send?
He felt like he was in a room locked
He was in a problem he could not mend

"O' All knowing, please forgive me" he said
"Please, anything but that you ask
I will fight those demons, till I am dead
For dying is the easier task

My son Rama is my soul
Sending him I cannot bear
Instead you take my life, as a whole
For I cannot send Rama there"

At Dasharatha the sage was at rage
But just then Vasishta Maharshi came
King Dasharatha was then advised by the sage,
"O' King, sage Vishwamitra's anger is a flame

Those monsters, the sage himself could kill

But he asked for Rama just to train

He asked for Rama to develop a skill

Trust me, sending him will not be in vain"

Upon these words, the king thought

Rama and Lakshmana he would send

They can then learn whatever the sage taught

This way their knowledge would extend

To Vishwamitra, the king then went

The king then touched the sage's feet

Rama and Lakshmana along with him were sent

Those two brothers, those demons cannot defeat

Powerful mantras to the brothers did he teach

With them they could never get tired or ill

Soon a forest did they then reach

There the sage trained them to hone their skill

Like that they travelled the forest through

And learnt everything the sage told

They did everything the sage wanted them to do

They believed all that knowledge to be gold

They walked and walked, mile by mile

They walked throughout the day and night

Stopping here and there once in a while

They went through forests dark and bright

They crossed rivers, lakes and many a pond

They crossed cities, towns and many a village

With the beautiful nature did they bond

Along their way, they met many a sage

Finally they reached a deep wood

A deep wood cruel and dark

In between such beauty it stood

Yet like the rest of the forest it did not spark

Then Vishwamitra, did Rama ask

"O' Sage, why is this forest like this?

Why is this land covered by this cruel mask?

Why does beauty, this land miss?

Then from Vishwamitra the answer came-

"O' Rama, this was in fact a beautiful land

But for its destruction, there is one to blame

Tataki is the curse this place had to withstand

O' Rama, I am ordering you now

Go and that demon, you destroy

That demon can only be destroyed by thou

Then only, again, can this land dwell in joy

To this, did Rama then respond

"O' Guru, that demon I shall surely kill

You are my guru and with respect to that bond

I can never ever go against your will"

Saying so, that demon's name did he shout
Soon Tataki grew angry and came
To jump on to Rama, she was about
But with his arrow, Rama took an aim

At her, the arrow, Rama then shot
The arrow went and her heart was slit
And then her fallen body, the earth caught
With that force did the ground almost split

Then to Rama, Vishwamitra said
"O' Rama, you have done a brave deed
Now finally we can all go ahead
For at last, this land has been finally freed"

Rama learnt from the sage, with devotion deep
And with love, taught the great sage
They soon crossed a valley low and steep
And then a reached a lovely cottage

Looking at that Rama spoke with bliss
"O' Guru, this is such a lovely place
If I blink, my eyes will surely miss
Every inch of this land filled with grace"

"Yes, Siddha ashram is the most pleasant
Thus I wanted to conduct my yagna here
Since once here Lord Vishnu was present
To you, Rama, this place is just as dear

O' Rama and Lakshmana" the sage said
"My prayer, you shall protect in this place
And defeat those monsters we all dread
Them away from here you shall chase

For six days, here you shall stay
For six whole days, our yagna you shall guard
Look out for those demons each day
For defeating those demons might be hard

For five days the brothers stood

Yet the demons did not come for days through

The yagna went on as peacefully as it could

While every corner was in the brothers' view

On the sixth day, the demons came this way

But Rama and Lakshmana were prepared for it

Rama soon defeated Maricha and threw him away

And the other demons did the brothers badly hit

The yagna was done without any mess

With that, were the sages very glad

With all their heart, them did they bless

They blessed them with all the wisdom they had

"O' Great brothers" said the sages as one

"For protecting our yagna, we must thank you

We thank you for this deed you have done

Indeed both of you are a Kshatriya true

Come with us to Mithila state

For a great yagna is conducted by the king

And king Janaka would feel more than great

You two, with us, if we shall bring

Moreover he has a magnificent bow

To lord Shiva, it is said to belong

To you, King Janaka would be happy to show

Hence, with us to Mithila, you come along"

They walked and walked for a long while

Then a beautiful ashram they came to

Its beauty would make anyone smile

But it seemed abandoned through and through

Rama asked, "O' Sage, why is this place so lone?

Though it retains its beauty and glow

Every corner of this, seems to be alone

O' Sage the reason for this, do you know?"

Vishwamitra then said, "Here once lived a lovely pair
Ahalya and Gautama were their names
People loyal like them were very rare
For their love, the proof were the flames

Lord Indra disguised as Gautama one day
And in front of Ahalya, he sat
Though she knew it, she did not say
Nor did she question Lord Indra for that

Because of this Gautama was outraged
And his own wife did he curse
'In this ashram you shall be caged
Till then I shall roam the Universe

You shall have only air as food
You shall stay here all alone
There is only one way your curse can conclude
And the way you can get back your flesh and bone

For one day, here, shall come a boy

He is Dasharatha's eldest son

Rama shall come, and your curse he will destroy

When he comes this curse shall be undone

Then only again, my hand you can gain

And I shall accept you as mine'

Saying so, he left her in this pain

O' Rama step on to this land divine

O' Rama please, right now, go in

From that curse, set Ahalya free

And let her get back her body and skin

For so long, she has been waiting for thee

As soon as Rama entered that place

To her human form did Ahalya return

And to that ashram returned its grace

And into the most beautiful ashram did it turn

Gautama finally came back to his wife
And accepted his Ahalya as his own
To the ashram returned its charm and life
And that land, finally, was no longer alone

Soon the brothers and the sages went ahead
And finally Mithila did they reach
Them to the palace, the king himself led
The king welcomed them all, one and each

While talking to the sages noticed the king
Two handsome princes did the king see
Them both, here, why did the sages bring
He couldn't make out, who they could be?

He asked, "O' Great sage, who are they?
To which kingdom do these princes belong?
They came here with you all the way
Is there a reason why they came along?"

Then did Vishwamitra reply,
"They are the sons of Kosala's king
From Ayodhya they came to the kingdom thy
For with me, to Mithila, them did I bring

To see the Shivadhanus they came with me
O' King, I want to show them the bow of thou
That majestic bow I wanted them to see
Thus, O' King can you get the Shivadhanus now?"

The sage's order did the king fulfil
To get the bow, ordered the king
Five thousand soldiers were pulling it, still
They found it difficult to bring

Finally they brought it close enough to show
The Shivadhanus did Rama then sight
Vishwamitra then said, "Lift the bow"
For he knows and has seen Rama's might

Rama did as the sage said

He lifted the bow with ease

He lifted it, and pulled up the thread

But it broke before he could release

King Janaka was astounded at this sight

He said, "An extraordinary scene did I just see

I have never seen someone with such might

O' Rama, there is no one stronger than thee

I have promised my daughter long ago

That the strongest man she shall wed

A soul stronger than you, I do not know

Thus to my daughter, Sita you shall tie the thread"

To Ayodhya messengers were soon sent

The king was pleased to hear the news

To Mithila, he and his queens soon went

In Mithila they were welcomed with many hues

There was a rain of petals to welcome the king

The decorations there seemed to touch the sky

Prayers and praises did the people sing

In such beauty, one couldn't blink an eye

Janaka's brother Kushadwaja welcomed them there

Like his brother, he also had daughters two

Of them, sages Vasishta and Vishwamitra were aware

About both the families the sages very well knew

Addressing the brothers, the sages then said,

"O' King Janaka as per your promise

Your daughter Sita, Sri Rama shall wed

They both shall live together in bliss

Your child Urmila with Lakshmana shall be

For they both are perfect for each other

O' Kushadwaja, with the permission of thee

Mandavi and Bharata shall be for one another

And Srutakirti, your daughter youngest
To her Shatrughna is an ideal groom
All of them to each other are the best
All their lives shall henceforth bloom"

With the elders' assent were the weddings planned
The whole city was shining like gold
Arrangements were made rich and grand
The city shone in colors bold

Soon came that special day
The weddings did both the sages guide
To the fire god did they then pray
While hundreds of sages followed alongside

Then King Janaka brought Sita there
In front of Rama did she then sit
The most beautiful jewels did she wear
Yet they were nothing to the charm she could emit

To Rama then Janaka fondly said,
"She is Sita, my daughter, my heart
With you from today, she shall be wed
You and she shall never be apart

She shall treat you like she god
You, she shall follow forever
She shall stay with you in any odd
She shall be with you whatsoever

She shall be your other half
May blessings shower from all the lands
O' Rama, be there for she on my behalf"
Saying so he put Sita in Rama's hands

The weddings of the couples other three
Were done with the same pomp and show
The weddings did the whole world see
It was the greatest celebration one could ever know

Rama and Sita were now husband and wife

Their wedding did the Fire God himself see

They both were now bonded for life

Forever, together they both shall be

Vishwamitra blessed the couples, the next day

He blessed each of them with all his heart

For them, to the Gods did the sage pray

Then his journey back to the Himalayas did he start

The same day Dasharatha took leave

All his family members with him

He was happier than he could ever believe

The joy in his face could never get dim

Many gifts with his daughters Janaka sent

He blessed them all throughout

Receiving those presents they all went

Towards Ayodhya did they set out

While to Ayodhya, they all were heading

Bharata and Shatrughna were heading elsewhere

They were going to Kekaya Kingdom after their wedding

Because Bharata's grandfather lives there

For Bharata, his grandfather wanted to meet

For that he sent Yudhaajit, his son

But when he arrived at Ayodhya no one came to greet

In the palace as well there were people none

In Mithila they were, he found out

So Yudhaajit too, decided to go there

But Bharata's wedding, he did not know about

Thus why they were there, he was not aware

He went to Dasharatha and then said,

"O' King, my father wants to see his grandson

Since he couldn't come, he sent me instead

So with me, please, send your son"

"Bharata is getting married today
Thus after his wedding, him I shall send
So till then, I wish for you to stay
And his wedding, I hope you attend"

Thus after the wedding, Bharata went
And with him Shatrughna came along
Their wives along with them, Kushadwaja sent
And they reached there after travelling for long

There with his uncle and granddad
Bharata lost track of time in joy
To stay there, they were very glad
Their happiness even God could not destroy

Meanwhile, Ayodhya, Rama was heading to
Along with all his family, he was going there
But just when they were crossing a forest through
Of a sage standing there, they became aware

Parashurama was this great sage's name

He came and challenged Rama outright

"You have broken the Shivadhanus you seem to claim

If so try to string this bow with all your might

For, to Lord Vishnu did this bow belong

No one except him and Lord Shiva can lift it"

Rama came and lifted the bow so strong

And with ease placed the string in its slit

Rama gracefully took an arrow and placed it right

"O' Parashurama, I have done what you told me to do"

Parashurama was astounded by Rama's might

He had done what was possible for a select few

"O' Rama, I have realized the might of thee

Astonishing feats today did you show

I have realized, O' Rama, you are the same as me"

Saying so did he bless Sri Rama and go

Rama then returned to the kingdom along with his dad
Of Ayodhya, Rama and Lakshmana took care
Such that no one in Kosala was sad
And each and every one was treated fair

With the time grew Sita and Rama's bond
They both loved each other more than anyone
Day by day for each other, they grew fond
Like that, they both had become one

Their love was like the starry sky
Where infinite stars shone with grace
If one measured their love, it was ever so high
Their love was as big as the infinite space

They lived happily for years through
Together did they both joyfully stay
The city did not fall in its hue
In fact, it grew brighter day by day

One day a decision, Dasharatha made

To crown Rama as the next king

He made this decision for people's aid

But he wanted to know what results it would bring

Thus his court did he then call

And asked "Rama I want to enthrone

I believe he is a king accepted by all

He is the most rightful to sit on this throne

Thus, tell me the advice of thee

Is the decision I took, right?

Your opinion, please tell me

Tell me with all your foresight"

For this the courtiers said as one

"O' Prabhu, we all agree with the decision thy

To be the king better than Rama are none

That truth, in this world, no one can deny"

Dasharatha was pleased with what they told

But the people's opinion he wanted to know

Ayodhya, how they think Rama would mould?

In Rama's hands how would Kosala grow?

To the people then Dasharatha went

"O' People, I want Rama to be the next king

For that, O' People, I seek your assent

Do you feel that this kingdom Rama can up bring?"

The people started applauding in delight

And all in one voice they said

"O' Prabhu, your decision is very right!

Your whole kingdom Rama will perfectly head

Rama is the best king any day

There is nothing that he cannot do

In fact, if you do not mind us say

Rama might be a better king than you"

Dasharatha felt happy with this
Arrangements of the crowning did he start
The kingdom was flooded with fun and bliss
In the fest each and every one took part

Happy with the results all
He knew they all would respond well
Rama did the king then call
Rama, Dasharatha decided to tell

When he came, the king told, "O' Rama welcome
I have decided to crown you as the king
The emperor I want you to become
And prosperity to this land you shall bring"

To Dasharatha then did Rama respond
"O' Father, your word is my command
I can never disrespect our bond
With all my life I shall take care of your land"

"O' Rama", Dasharatha then replied
"Tomorrow is a very nice day,
Your crowning shall be celebrated nationwide
O' Rama, go to Kausalya and this good news you say"

To Kausalya's palace did he and Sita go
Even Lakshmana and Sumitra were there in her room
After hearing the news their faces were aglow
Because of Rama's crowning did their hearts bloom

Kausalya blessed them with all her heart
Sumitra blessed Sita and Rama too
"O' Rama as a great king, may your life start
Live to be a king, wise and true"

To his mothers then Rama replied,
"O' Mothers, thank you for the blessings of thee
I shall never fail with my dear brothers beside
A king like father, I shall try my best to be"

To Lakshmana, he said, "O' Brother, you are my right arm

I wish to share all my pleasures with you

O' Lakshmana, we four brothers are this kingdom's charm

Together there is nothing we cannot do"

About the crowning, they were all dwelling in joy

The people were celebrating all festivals in one

For the crowning ceremony did they all enjoy

There, the people unhappy were none

Manthara was Kaikeyi's maid

Since Kaikeyi was born, with her, she was there

After Kaikeyi's marriage with her only she stayed

There also, of Kaikeyi she took care

That day she looked at the city

And saw its charm and glory

She wondered why the place was so pretty

She wondered, behind it what was the story

One of Kausalya's maids did she enquire
"Why is the city charming so bright?
Is there a news, I have to admire?
Why is the city emitting such light?"

The answer then came from the maid
"Don't you know, Rama will be the next king?
Tomorrow, the crowned prince, he will be made
Prosperity to this land he will surely bring"

At this Manthara was shocked
To Kaikeyi's chamber, she soon ran
She went and her door she knocked
And as soon as she entered, she began

"O' Queen, the news is bad,
Rama, tomorrow will be crowned
O' Queen, for you I feel so sad"
Saying so she deeply frowned

To her then came Kaikeyi's reply
"O' Maid, why are you so blue?
You are glum at this time I do not know why
At such blissful time what happened to you?

To be the king, Rama is the one
There is nothing that he cannot do
Better than Rama there is none
Rama surely is a Kshatriya true!"

Manthara snapped, "Don't be a fool
Bharata should be the king
In this danger how can you be so cool?
I wonder if you know a thing

If as the king, Rama is crowned
The queen Kausalya will become
To her power, there shall be no bound
If so, our destruction shall soon come-"

"O' Foolish woman, you have mistaken
For Rama, equal are we three
Listening to me I hope you have awaken
For Rama to be the king, I totally agree"

"Kaikeyi, you do not understand
If he is the king, he will ignore your son
He will be the one to rule this land
You and Bharata, he will surely abandon"

With that did Kaikeyi go blind
In hatred's pit did she dwell
About Rama, she changed her mind
And into Manthara's trap she fell

"O' Manthara," she stuttered and said,
"What do you think I should do?
This kingdom I want my son to head
The only one to answer is you!"

Delighted at the triumph of her plot,

She said, "O' Queen, I have a plan –

Remind the king of the time he forgot

When to save his life, you did all you can

Indra and Sambarasa were at war, long ago

Of Lord Indra, your king took side

In that battle he received a fatal blow

And without you, he would have surely died

From danger, you took him away

You were the one who kept him alive

Because of you, he is living today

Only because of you, did he survive

Thus for your bravery, the king gave you

Two boons for your brave deed

With them, then, you didn't know what to do

Now is the best time to ask those boons indeed"

That idea, did Kaikeyi then use
She waited in her room for her king
To wear her jewels did she refuse
She looked gloomy and said not a thing

Dasharatha then came to her room
About the crowning, to Kaikeyi he wanted to tell
But when he entered she was in gloom
It looked as if that room was in hell

He asked, "O' Dear, why are you sad?
What has happened to you?
It seems like your day went bad
Is there anything for me to do?"

"O' Prabhu" did she then speak
"This day is very glum for me
There is something that I truly seek
And that can only be given by thee"

The king said, "Whatever it is my dear,
I will get anything for you
You want to visit a place far or near?
For you, that also I shall do

You wish a prisoner to be freed?
That also will surely be done
Ten thousand people you wish to feed?
You, those arrangements shall stun"

"O' Prabhu," Kaikeyi spoke in a flash
"None of them, do I now seek
Do you remember in that terrible clash
I saved you when you were weak

Then you gave me wishes two
That I still did not ask till now
With them I now know, what to do
Those boons I wish to ask thou"

"O' Love," Dasharatha smiled and said
"You know, as my beloved wife
You know as the person whom I have wed
That my eldest son Rama, is my life

~

On him I shall make my vow
That all you ask I shall fulfil
Whatever you wish, you tell me now
I wish to do all I can and I will"

~

Delighted that he fell into her plot
She said, "O' Lord, as my king you know
That I love my son Bharata a lot
Hence I shall ask you my wishes as you say so

~

As the first wish that I place before the rest
Bharata as the king I wish to see
And Rama for fourteen years to live in a forest
My second wish that shall be"

~

Dasharatha, himself, he seemed to forget

He thought, "Is this a dream?

Making that promise, do I now regret

This, I cannot believe, Kaikeyi could scheme"

Later, himself did he find

"Kaikeyi, is this truly you?

Are you in your state of mind?

I can't believe, this, you can do

Rama you love, I heard you say

To those words, what has happened

Has the night replaced the day

Better than this, my life, you end"

"O' King, is this what you will do?

Like this, prosperity to this land, how will you bring?

Like this you cannot be an emperor true

Shouldn't you follow Dharma as the king?"

"O' Kaikeyi, I beg you
Do not take my life away
Rama is this kingdom's hue
I beg you, O' Kaikeyi, please obey"

Saying so, Dasharatha touched her feet
But Kaikeyi instantly drew them away
With that promise, his people, how will he meet?
He prayed for the time to not move but stay

But the time was time and it had to move
The night had soon become the day
The dark blanket did the sky remove
People soon got up and for Rama did they pray

They were all waiting for Rama and the king
Then into the court Vasishta Maharshi came
For the crowning he prepared everything
In the preparations there were no flaws to blame

For the king, Sumantra, the sage then sent

Of Dasharatha, he was a subject loyal

To the palace then Sumantra went

And entered Kaikeyi's chamber royal

In the room the king looked very weak

In the room, he sat with eyes red

In that glum, he couldn't even speak

Thus Kaikeyi then spoke instead

Rama, she asked Sumantra to bring,

Thus to Rama's chambers did he go

There Sita and Rama were sitting on a swing

Talking to each other while the wind swept slow

"O' Prince," Sumantra then said

"Your father, the king, is calling thee

Thus to your chamber did I head

O' Rama, hence please come with me"

Rama agreed and as he came out of his room

Exploded the people's cheers and praise

Like a flower did the whole city bloom

The city blossomed like a lotus upon the rays

Rama's chariot did Lakshmana ride

Towards the king's chamber did they go

Rama's name echoed from every side

Like stars the people's hearts were aglow

He was the kingdom's mind and might

He was Ayodhya's shine and hue

He was his people's hope and light

He was their beloved leader new

Rama was loved by each and everyone

For him cheered the kingdom whole

He was the gemstone of the clan of sun

Of Kosala he was the life and soul

Prayers for Rama did the people sing

He was admired by every man, woman and child

From all the ten sides did his praises ring

At all of their love Rama then smiled

Rama addressed the people one and each

He spoke to all of them, all through the way

The palace did they soon reach

They then went to their father soon away

They then came into Kaikeyi's room

Dasharatha was still in deep dismay

Still immersed in all that gloom

"Rama!" was all he was able say

Ignoring Dasharatha, Kaikeyi then said,

"Rama, your father has given me a promise

Now, he is dodging that word instead

As the king, what kind of Dharma is this?

When I asked him for my wish last night
He told me, he would do anything that I say
Thus I asked him, my wish outright
Now from his word he wants to get away"

To her did Rama then reply,
"Your wish, O' Mother, please tell me
I shall surely fulfil the wish thy
I will fulfil it, no matter what it may be"

Then to Rama did Kaikeyi say
"Rama, promise me, my wish you shall fulfil
Until then, here only I shall stay
If you don't, it shall remain a disgrace to your skill"

To Kaikeyi, his word Rama gave
Of her boons he was not aware
Kaikeyi then asked her boons grave
Her boons did Kaikeyi then declare

Pleased with what she has done,

She said, "Rama, I have my wishes two,

First, this kingdom, Bharata should run

Second, go to the forest for fourteen years through"

Kaikeyi's wishes did Rama hear

Yet he remained ever so calm

With his eyes still crystal clear

On Kaikeyi's feet he placed his palm

"O' Mother, are these the wishes of thee?

Father took all the trouble for this?

About this you could have simply told me

I would have fulfilled your wishes with bliss"

Kaikeyi was half shocked, half glad

While Dasharatha's heart screamed in pain

Kaikeyi got the kingdom for her lad

While Dasharatha felt the hues drain

Rama then said, "O' Mother, Ma Kausalya, let me see
After seeing her, I shall take leave of you
I shall leave the kingdom for Bharata and thee
I will live in exile, as long as you told me to"

Taking leave of her, Rama left the room
Kaikeyi looked like she just touched the sky
Dasharatha was destroyed in that gloom
He knelt to the ground and began to cry

All through the talk, Lakshmana stood,
He stood listening, calm and still
Insides in rage, yet he kept as calm as he could
Yet his insides were screaming loud and shrill

Rama then reached Kausalya's room
Kausalya was pleased to see Rama there
The room was filled with sandal perfume
Of what had happened she was still unaware

Rama touched her feet and then said,

"O' Mother, there is something you need to know

Of Ayodhya, Bharata is the new king instead

And for fourteen years to the forest I must go"

Listening to Rama, she fell to the ground

In grief, her heart screamed and cried

Cruel darkness was filled all around

And slowly it was seeping inside

She sobbed, "O' Rama, don't leave, I beg you

If you leave I have nothing but to die

If you leave I will drown in this blue"

Clenching her heart she began to cry

Rama said, "O' Mother, don't say such a thing

My father is the king to one and all

And I must do what I was told by my king

And fourteen years is a time so small"

"O' Rama, then with you I shall also come

With you I will also bear all that pain

For it is better than bearing all this glum

Without you, all around, the hues will drain

To the sages who visit, food I shall give

I shall sleep there on the floor without a bed

With you only, fourteen years I shall live

Without you, Rama, I shall better be dead"

Rama replied, "O' Mother, do not say so

That cruel forest, your body cannot bear

You cannot live in a forest so low

It easier for you stay here than there"

She replied, "Since Sumitra and Kaikeyi have come

I was deprived of the love from my king

Though I was older, least wanted, I had become

His ignorance to me, till date does it sting

My existence the king long forgot

Through years I just lived like a statue

But life back to me, your birth has brought

Now, Rama, what will I do without you?

O' Rama, you are the eldest son

Even with you, this is my state

O' Rama, if me you abandon,

Imagine, what shall be my fate"

Her words Lakshmana couldn't withstand

Clenching his fists, he exclaimed in rage,

"O' Rama, only you deserve to rule this land

O' Rama, a war against the king, let us wage

For Kaikeyi no need to stoop so low

No need to stoop so low, while I am there

Our strength to Kaikeyi let us show

And crown yourself as the king's true heir

Do not forget the powers of you and me

I can outwit our soldiers with a single hand

O' Brother, to my plan please agree

In moments they shall all turn to sand"

He and Kausalya were on the same page

But with them Rama couldn't reason

He said, "O' Lakshmana, control your rage

How can a father be attacked by his own son

Anger is covering you like a cloud of smoke

Calm down, O' Brother, then you will know

You will understand the words you just spoke

That he is our revered father and not our foe"

Within a second Lakshmana replied

"O' Brother, no need to fulfil that woman's demand

Why, in this, are you taking her side?

Think again, O' Rama, I am at your command

You tell me once, you will be the king

You tell me once, to the forest you will never go

You tell me once, the moon I shall bring

You tell me once, like the day, the night shall glow"

Rama wanted him to understand,

Hence he said, "O' Brother, this is wrong

Ma Kaikeyi has our father's hand

And like a mother, she also raised us all along"

Lakshmana said, "O' Rama, I am telling you

If you ever go to exile, before you I shall stand

If you ever jump into fire, before thee, I shall too

All the pain, you ever bear, I also shall withstand"

Rama said, "O' Lakshmana, I told you

I am going to the forest by my own will

Thus there is no need for you to be blue

With my choice, her wishes, I want to fulfil

The wish of God, I believe it is

Because of that, I was ordered by the king

If not this day wouldn't be like this

For Ma Kaikeyi would never do such a thing

She loved us four brothers the same

I have always loved her like my mother own

From father such boons, she would never claim

For Bharata she wouldn't have asked the throne

But Father's word can never be denied

Bharata shall be the king new

And in a forest, I shall go and reside

For my father, this, I am willing to do"

Both Kausalya and Lakshmana were sad

They so hoped for Rama to stay

The only little hope that they had

Like a tide, it had been washed away

They both agreed with Rama at the end
To Sita, did Rama and Lakshmana then go
They needed to tell her what happened
About what happened, she also had to know

For Rama, Sita was waiting there
She wondered why that day felt so grey
Of all that happened she was unaware
She was unaware of what happened that day

When Rama came, she asked him,
"O' Rama, I wonder why this day is so low
I don't know why today feels so grim
Is there something I do not know?"

To Sita, Rama told everything
He told her of Kaikeyi's boon
"Thus Bharata shall be the new king
And to the forest, I shall leave soon

O' Sita, to the forest I have to go

And I do not wish to take you there

I don't want you to live there so low

For, seeing you like that I cannot bear

If you stay back, you will be happier

Staying in the palace is safer for you

Thus it is better for you to stay here

In the palace you will have troubles few

Till I come back, in this palace, you stay

After my exile I will come back to thee

Take care of my parents while I am away

O' Sita, there is no need to worry about me"

Sita replied, "O' Rama, living in a forest is tough

But living without you is more

Snakes, insects, lions, I will bear all that stuff

Just to stay with you, whom I adore

Only a coward can the troubles scare
But Sri Rama's wife they cannot
I will never be afraid, if you are there
Coming with you is my duty to our knot

My father, King Janaka, gave me to you
I am yours from then, I am yours forever
My love for you, was, and will remain true
So I shall follow your footsteps whatsoever

As a wife I never asked you a thing
O' Rama, my only wish is to be with you
To me, you are, forever the king
With you, to the forest I shall come too"

Rama told her to not come along
To convince her, he tried and tried
He tried to convince her for so long
But whatever he told, she always denied

She then said, "O' Rama, please,

Please do not bother about me

I can withstand that forest with ease

But I cannot bear a day without thee

My world revolves around you

Yet, here, you want to leave me

Without you, O' Rama, my world is blue

For me to come with you, please agree

With you, a forest is a temple

With you, a thorn seems to bloom

With you, any trouble seems simple

With you, I can fight any gloom

Without you, Rama, the world is glum

I wish to walk with you, holding your hand

O' Rama, with you, please let me come

Not being with you, I cannot withstand"

Sita was sad that Rama had vowed

Vowed to encourage Kaikeyi's pride

Sorrow engulfed her like a cloud

Hugging Rama, she silently cried

Looking at her, did Rama smile

And said, "O' Sita, you can come with me

Holding your hand, I shall walk every mile

Every single day, you I shall see

Sita, without you I cannot imagine my life

With you, any problem, I can go through

O' Sita, I am blessed to have you as my wife

O' Sita, I will never go anywhere without you"

With that, Sita's glum had ended

Now Sita, no longer felt so low

Her broken heart was now mended

With her Rama, she could also go

Lakshmana then touched Rama's feet

And said, "O' Brother, let me also come

Like my parents, you both, I shall treat

A servant to you both, I shall become

O' Rama, you are the dearest to me

You, I always place before the rest

I do not wish to live without thee

Please, let me also come to the forest"

Rama agreed for him to come as well

"O' Lakshmana, to Vasishta Maharshi you go

Of all that has happened to him you tell

All that happened he needs to know

Sita's father had given us bows two

Now, the Maharshi has them with him

They will help, as we travel the forest through

With them, we can face any danger grim

Lakshmana bought those bows as Rama said

To those bows, the rites Sita then did

Then to Dasharatha's place did they head

As to him, farewell they have to bid

They headed to his place to say goodbye

For soon after, for the forest will they leave

For Sri Rama's exile did the whole city cry

For their exile did entire Ayodhya grieve

To Dasharatha's room they went on their feet

About Rama's exile, Ayodhya got to know

As they walked, people rushed to the street

As Rama left, so did Ayodhya's glow

They followed Rama all through the way

People came to him from all over the land

They begged and pleaded for Rama to stay

But on his word did Rama firmly stand

They soon reached Dasharatha's room
His three wives were there with him
Except Kaikeyi all were filled with gloom
Except Kaikeyi all others were grim

Rama touched his father's feet and said
"O' Father, I shall be leaving to the forest
Bharata shall replace me as the king instead
But, O' Father I have but one request

Sita and Lakshmana want to come with me
Without them I cannot live through a day
Hence, O' Father, if it is fine by thee
With me in the forest, they both shall stay"

"O' Rama, to the forest, you do not have to go
You can slay me here and attain the throne
Me, with your strength you can easily out throw
Without you, Ayodhya shall wither alone

I have given my word; I must do what I say

But unlike me, Rama, you are not chained

Outplaying me, why don't you stay?

The throne, O' Rama can still be attained"

"O' Father," Rama then replied,

"What you said can never be done

Your words, I shall always abide

For the father's word is the duty of a son

For me, O' Father, do not feel so low

Take care of my three mothers instead

For fourteen years to the forest I will go

And live peacefully under nature's shed"

"O' Rama, at least stay for one day

Spend this day with Kausalya and me

Enjoy the royalty while you stay

O' Rama, at least accept this plea"

Rama replied, "O' Father, thank you
But today itself, to the forest I shall go
O' Father, for me, don't remain blue
O' Father, for me, do not feel so low

I will leave those luxuries for the new king
As my brother, Bharata is a part of my soul
Him or me enjoying them, is the same thing
He will also take care of this kingdom whole"

Such anger Sumantra couldn't hold for long
As he shouted at Kaikeyi, his post, he forgot
"Kaikeyi, what you are doing is wrong!
With greed your thoughts have started to rot!"

The king did nothing in his despair
For Kaikeyi to change, he had little hope
Because whatsoever Kaikeyi did not care
With the wound in his heart, he couldn't cope

Then Sumantra did Dasharatha call
"Prepare our troops to go with my son
Carts filled with goods you install
For Rama's comfort, do all that is to be done

Send guards with him, who shall guard all night
Send architects who shall build a palace there
Rama should not feel a discomfort slight
Of Rama's every need you must take care

With him send servants of every skill
Who can do all that is required for him
All of his needs and wishes you fulfil
In that forest he should never be grim

Build another Ayodhya in the forest
Use as much gold as needed for this
Everything over there must be the best
It should be perfect for him to live in bliss"

Kaikeyi then interrupted the king
"You are sending away grains and gold
For Bharata you haven't left a thing
I don't need a kingdom so dry and cold"

How low could she stoop with her greed
By her, astounded, were the people there
All were cursing her for her misdeed
Yet Kaikeyi wasn't moved by a hair

Dasharatha then said that he would also go
Go to and live with his beloved son
Rama replied, "O' Father don't feel so low
Your people at this time you shouldn't abandon

For Bharata, I am leaving the kingdom entire
Is it so hard to leave those luxuries behind?
O' Father, none of those do I desire
All that I need, in the forest, I can find

With all this wealth, let Ayodhya be

The forest already has all I need

When nature herself will take care of me

O' Father, you do not have to do such a deed"

Kaikeyi was gleeful with what Rama told

About what others thought, she did not care

For her son, she defended all the gold

And she herself got the clothes for them to wear

The clothes to them did she then hand

Taking those, to get ready, they went

Felt sorry looking at them, the entire land

For them did the entire Ayodhya lament

They soon got ready to leave

To Dasharatha did they then go

For Rama, did all of them grieve

For without him, Kosala loses its glow

People ran after him, begging him to stay

Even children were calling out to him

All of them, were in deep dismay

As Rama left, the land grew dim

Vasishta Maharshi always had control over his rage

But this time, at Kaikeyi he lost his grip

And said, "Kaikeyi! Your actions can anger a sage

This family apart why do you seek to rip?

To Ikshvaku's dynasty, you are a scar

You have hurt both the kingdom and the king

To even remorse, you have taken this too far

Don't you know the results your actions bring?

Following Rama, people will leave this land

With Rama, everyone here, shall leave

In this kingdom only you will stand

Then only you alone shall stay and grieve

Here, you alone shall reside

Only you shall live in this lifeless place

You won't find a soul living by your side

Except yours, you won't see a face

If Rama isn't here, this is no longer a kingdom

It is no longer a kingdom, however great it may be

This place is nothing without his strength and wisdom

At least now, understand the crimes done by thee

Did you not think about what Bharata would say?

Did you not think about your son before you began?

Did you really think that for this, Bharata would obey?

Did you forget that he is also from the same clan?

Kaikeyi, without planning, you kept your hopes high

Now look at the destruction you have done

He will never accept this, even if you jump till the sky

Bharata will not accept this, even if on water, you run

I will now tell you, what is sure to come

Bharata and Shatrughna shall wear clothes of cotton

They will also go with Rama, and live without glum

You shall stay here alone and long forgotten

Sita shall never wear cotton clothes in her life

She would wear the silk ones everyday

She would wear jewels worth of Rama's wife

Forever here in Ayodhya, they shall stay"

Even for the sage's words, Kaikeyi didn't care

To care for them she was way too blind

Cursing her, were all the people there

But even their words she did not mind

The three then soon prepared to leave

Like that, Kausalya couldn't see her son

For Rama, did Kausalya deeply grieve

Without Rama, there was joy none

She still hoped that Rama would stay

Without Rama, her life would only grow dim

Without him, she couldn't live through a day

For her, there was no reason to live without him

Lakshmana then touched Sumitra's feet

Sumitra blessed him with all her heart

Her tears even she couldn't defeat

With her sons she did not want to part

But as a queen she shouldn't feel so low

And her duties she cannot abandon

Thus her emotions did she swallow

Still controlling them, she spoke to her son

"O' Son, Rama is your father from today

And your mother Sita shall be

As your Gods, to them you pray

In them, Vishnu and Lakshmi you see"

All three of them did she then bless
Sumantra's chariot they then got onto
Their tears none of them could suppress
As the whole city was left in blue

For Ayodhya it was the darkest day
A darkness, that can't be washed, even by the sun
They couldn't bear to see their prince, going away
Hence, behind the chariot did many run

The people's sorrow, Dasharatha saw
He couldn't bear it, hence he cried
"O' Sumantra, the chariot, back you draw!
Without Rama I feel like I have died!"

To turn back the chariot, did Sumantra try
But Rama told him to stay on the track
Begging him to return, did Ayodhya cry
But Rama left, never once turning back

Dasharatha couldn't believe what he had seen

With his own hands, he sent his life away

Tears poured out, from deep within

As his life turned a hue-less grey

He felt like he could never escape this glum

He felt like the earth had turned to hell

Dasharatha felt his feet going numb

As onto the ground, the king fell

After he woke up, to Kaikeyi, he said,

"Kaikeyi, please stay away from me!

My life, into a thousand pieces you have shred

For such vengeance, what did I do to thee?

As my wife, I have always loved you

I always loved you, with all my heart

Wasn't my love for you, always true?

That you wished to rip my soul apart"

The king told Kaikeyi not to come near him
And to Kausalya's chamber, did he go
About that day, they both were grim
They both had lost their life's glow

On the chariot, travelling, were the three
Behind them did whole of Ayodhya come
With Rama only, they wanted to be
Without him, they could never bear that glum

Rama felt that them coming, was wrong
So he said, "O' Sumantra, please stop
It is not fair for the people to come along
Hence, us three, here only you drop"

As told by Rama, Sumantra did
All the people had to leave them there
To the three, goodbye they all bid
The three then left, leaving the people in despair

From there, on feet they then went

After some time, a forest did they come to

Under a tree, they arranged a small tent

There, they decided to spend the night through

As they were setting their tent there

A horse galloping they could hear

They couldn't see it in the moonlight bare

But they knew it was coming near

On that horse did Guha ride

He was the chief of that forest

Close by did his tribe reside

He came there to welcome his guest

Who Guha was, Rama knew

They both were friends from long ago

Soon Guha came into their view

To embrace him, did Rama himself go

Delighted with them, Guha then said,
"O' Rama, I got to know what happened to thee
But you three can happily stay here instead
You can happily stay with my tribe and me

O' Rama, for fourteen years live here
And for leaving Ayodhya, don't be sad
Like this, to your home, you will stay near
For you to stay here, we are more than glad"

"O' Guha, thank you," Rama replied
"But here, with you all I cannot stay
For the rules of exile, I must abide
Hence into the deep forest, I must go away"

About the rules of exile, Guha was aware
Thus Rama couldn't agree to Guha's plea
Guha was sad that they couldn't stay there
But to Rama's words he had to agree

Back to his tribe soon Guha went

He rode his horse back into the forest deep

Sita and Rama left to sleep in the tent

But Lakshmana did not feel like falling asleep

Sita and Rama soon fell asleep inside

But Lakshmana stood outside, wide awake

In front of him, he burnt a few twigs dried

With them, a small bonfire did he make

He sat on guard as he wore his bow

Guha also then came, with his weapons clad

He sat beside Lakshmana in the fire's glow

He knew that for Rama, Lakshmana was sad

Guha then said, "O' Lakshmana, why?

Why do you want to take this trouble?

Go, sleep peacefully under this starry sky

To protect you three, my forces, I shall double

I am telling you now, what I know is true

Rama has been and will be my dearest friend

So, it is my duty to protect them and you

Hence go and sleep while I stay here to defend"

"O' Guha, they both should be in their palace room

Yet, here, they are sleeping on the forest floor

To deserve this, they have done misdeeds to whom?

O' Guha, in this glum I cannot sleep anymore

For all the prayers that my father did

Rama was the blessing that the Gods gave

Rama was talented even as a kid

He is man, smart, talented, kind and brave

My father and mothers adored him

They loved him more than anyone

In front of his charm, even the sun is dim

In everything, he was second to none

I am worried for my parents, if anything
I am not sure they can bear this glum
Ayodhya will suffer if he isn't the king
I am afraid of what the kingdom will become

After returning home, after fourteen years
I won't see my father, I am afraid
Thinking of this, I am clouded by tears
Out of me, my happiness seems to fade"

Both of them guarded that night
They both spent that night in despair
About that day nothing was right
Seeing Sita and Rama like that, neither could bear

They woke up early the next day
Rama told that Ganga, he wanted to cross
He wanted to cross and reach the other bay
So as to reach that forest across

Hence to make a boat, Guha called his men
They soon made a boat, as Guha said
The three climbed onto the boat then
And the boat to the other shore, Guha led

Here, in Ayodhya everyone was sad
People were mourning, people were glum
Without Rama, they lost all the joy they ever had
Such a blue place Ayodhya had become

That night Kausalya was called by the king
To Dasharatha's room, did Kausalya then go
Though she was angry, she couldn't say a thing
She couldn't scold the king when he was so low

She strived to keep her heart intact
Her dear son was far away
Her heart ached with that ugly fact
Then, to Dasharatha, did she say

"O' Prabhu", she said, her eyes leaking a drop
"Kaikeyi has become a curse to you and me
She is a monster and by no means could she stop
She doesn't even wish to give respect to thee

Just when Rama was born, you could have given,
Given him as a servant to her dangerous mind
That way at least he would have been forgiven
That way at least he could have stayed behind"

In front of Dasharatha did Kausalya cry
He couldn't console her, when he himself was sad
Even to pour out, his eyes had gone dry
In his life, he had never seen a day so bad

Here, finally, the three reached the other shore
To the north of Ganga was a deep wood
It was so dense that no one could see the floor
There mighty, dark and deep it stood

Rama said, "Our exile now, has just begun
The forests are usually uninhabited and lone
But deep in there we might see someone
But most of the time we are alone"

They walked and walked throughout the day
Lakshmana in front, to direct the road
Behind him Sita walked along the way
And to protect her, behind Sita, Rama strode

A flat land near, they soon found
They decided to halt there at night
They spread some hay as a bed on the ground
Tired, Sita soon slept, under the moonlight

But somehow, Rama could not fall asleep that day
He said, "O' Lakshmana, another day has gone
In our long journey, a small part, is done today
And another one is to begin by tomorrow's dawn

In Ayodhya, my thoughts always lie

Do you think our parents are fine?

All I know is that we are under the same sky

Will I be able to see them after this exile mine?

For me to see our parents once more,

I have fourteen more years to go

But you have every chance to see them before

You should have left me long ago"

Listening to Rama, Lakshmana said,

"O' Brother, do not say that, please,

Leaving you, O' Rama, is all I dread

Away from you, I can never be at ease

O' Rama, for me and Ma Sita you are our life

If away from you, we shall surely die

After all, I am your brother and Ma Sita is your wife

On you, our lives, completely rely

Seeing our mothers, father or heaven, alone

Can never, ever be blissful without thee

As a child, holding your hand, I have grown

Do not ever think of leaving Ma Sita or me"

His brother's love, did Rama truly feel

He finally agreed to Lakshmana's reply

All of Rama's glum, he seemed to heal

Both of them soon slept, looking at the sky

The next day, their journey, did they continue

They walked on the curvy forest road

As they were walking, a hut came into view

It was Bharadwaja Maharishi's peaceful abode

To welcome them, he was more than glad

He served them, in all the ways he could

Hearing the news about Rama, he too was sad

He asked Rama to stay here, than in that dark wood

Respectfully, that advice, did Rama decline

Saying, "O' Maharshi, your advice, I must deny

For I must live in a forest through the exile mine

Thus I should not live in the ashram thy

But, O' Knowing sir, please help me

To live alone, is there a place you know?

Tell me a place that is known to thee

Soon to that place, we three shall go."

The sage replied, "O' Rama, I do know a place

After Chitrakoota Mountain a forest is there

That forest is lone yet full of grace

Finding such a place is, sure is, rare"

To where the sage said, they left the next day

Taking the sage's blessings, they left soon

Till the mountain they walked all the way

They walked for days, under the sun and moon

They found the forest behind the mountain
By Rama, to build a hut, Lakshmana was told
He built a handsome hut on a ground plain
It could protect them from the rain, heat and cold

For fourteen years, there, they decided to stay
It was a land so beautiful and serene
Such life and greenery did that place display
Its beauty was such, never before seen

To Ayodhya, Sumantra returned; his chariot void
With that terrible grief Ayodhya was blue
Without Rama their hearts were totally destroyed
Every second without Rama, their glum grew

To Dasharatha then did Sumantra go
With tear-bound eyes he looked at the king
From the king's eyes left the remaining glow
To his life did Dasharatha barely cling

Looking at Sumantra, he then said
"O' Sumantra, take me back to my son
Without Rama, it is better to be dead
With my own hands, such a crime I have done

Listening to my cruel wife
I, myself, sent my bliss away
I sent away my son, my soul, my life
Without him I am to remain grey

Thus O' Sumantra, I beg thou
From this crippling guilt, set me free
Take me to my Rama right now
And thus pour back the life into me

Even Kausalya requested him
She requested him to take her there
Without Rama they both were very grim
The absence of their son, they couldn't bear

Sumantra couldn't bear to see the king cry

About their son, they both wanted to know

But Sumantra couldn't bring himself to reply

He thus walked out, his head hanging low

To Dasharatha, then Kausalya said

"O' Prabhu, you are known to be kind

For years this kingdom you have led

But for your own son, you've turned blind

In the name of Dharma you sent away my son

What Dharma tells you to banish a boy?

What Dharma tells that Rama you should abandon?

What Dharma tells that a kingdom you should destroy?

My daughter Sita also had to go with him

What crimes of her made her go through this?

What crime of her led to a life so grim?

What crimes of her robbed her of all her bliss?

Years ago, you left me alone

For your love I had to strive

He was the only light God had shown

Only with his love, was I alive

O' Lord, you could've severed my head

But you sent away my life, our son

O' Prabhu I would've been happier if I were dead

For to live, his presence was my only reason

You are famous across the worlds three

You have done deeds worthy of the greatest king

You have answered each and everyone's plea

But you have lost all of that with a single thing"

In that glum, the king himself did she scold

Dasharatha listened to Kausalya's heartbreak

He couldn't blame Kausalya for what she told

For the king knew it was his own mistake

His heart and soul did her words slit

Yet he knew that all she was saying was true

Listening to all her cries did he just sit

Letting her pour her heart out was all he could do

"O' Kausalya, you were never angry on anyone

You have never spoken like this, until today

Yet I know I deserve that for what I have done

I knew long ago that I had to see this day

Those were the days before I met you

I had just learnt to hunt by the sound

That day it was raining all the way through

I went near the Sarayu River and sat on the ground

My ears to the ground did I link

I could hear the distant waters flow

Hoping to spot an elephant drink

I sat there ready, with my bow

I then heard someone move, I thought
Hence instantly I shot an arrow that way
But it was a human that my arrow had shot
Bleeding all over, on the ground did he lay

I ran to that person in hope to save
He happened to be a young sage
The sin that I had done was so grave
I was half prepared to bear his rage

But, he was not angry, to my surprise
Just lying there he then softly said
'O' Prince, do me one help after my demise
Please go and tell my parents that I am dead

My parents, who are old and blind,
To get some water, they sent me
For me, O' Revered prince, do be kind
Give them water, for it is my only plea'

Lying in my hands, he passed away

I felt the stopping of his heart

To his parents I then searched my way

I went to them, to do my part

I took some water as per his desire

Giving it to them, I told them of their son

It felt as if I set their hearts on fire

I knew it was the gravest sin I have done

Such a sudden shock they could not bear

For they were silent for a time so long

Then his father asked me to take him there

Thus to the riverside I took them along

Their loss was something I could never replace

And from such regret, I could never hide

They bent to try and feel their child's face

And hugging their son, they both cried

The father then in anger, cursed me
And said, 'Such a terrible sin did you commit
From this curse you shall never flee
I am telling you, O' Sinner, you shall pay for it

With the sorrow of my son's death, I will die
Like me, you will also die when your sons are away'
O' Kausalya, this curse I can never defy!
O' Kausalya, of destiny, I am but a small prey"

Saying so, Dasharatha took his final breath
Kausalya saw him and started to sob
She couldn't bear her husband's death
Of all of her happiness, God seemed to rob

Hearing her cries, Sumitra and Kaikeyi came in
They both were shocked about the king's death
The other two cursed Kaikeyi for her terrible sin
While they both wept trying to control their breath

Vasishta Maharshi soon got to know
He too was sad that the king is no more
He said, "It is gruesome that he had to go
When with him, there aren't his sons four"

He too blamed Kaikeyi for what she had done
For if not for her, the king would have been alive
And because of her, he had to die without a son
And his last rites had to wait until they arrive

He then called the king's servants and said
"Go to Kekaya kingdom and Bharata you call
Speak nothing of Rama or that the king is dead
Show no hint of glum, show nothing at all

Tell him that I have told him to come
Till then, the king's body must remain
We shall keep his body in an oil filled drum
After Bharata comes, everything, I shall explain"

The servants were quick, loyal and true
Thus soon for Bharata did they go
They rode the rivers and forests through
They rode through deserts and rode through snow

The servants reached Bharata within a few days
When they met, they told him the Maharishi's call
They led him to Ayodhya in the shortest of ways
They soon reached Ayodhya in no time at all

As soon as he reached, Ayodhya was blue
Sadness was etched on every face
The land was dry and had lost its hue
From Ayodhya, was pulled out, all its grace

When he reached, he went to Kaikeyi's room
When he entered, she was sitting there
Looking at her son, she seemed to bloom
Of all that happened, he was unaware

"Welcome home, O' Bharata, my lad!
My little son, how tall you grew!
Tell me about all the fun time you had
After all this time, how are you?"

"O' Mother Kaikeyi, I am very fine
But what happened here while I was gone?
Ayodhya seemed to lose every bit of her shine
It seems like here, the sun would never dawn"

About the king's death Kaikeyi told him,
He couldn't believe that the king is no more
About the king's death, he felt very grim
He regretted that he couldn't come before

"O' Mother, after father is dead
My brother Rama is now my king
He is the one to take Ayodhya ahead
The lost glory of this land, he shall bring"

"O' Bharata, no", Kaikeyi then told

"Rama happens to be in exile right now

The crown right now, only you can hold

Thus the king of Ayodhya has to be thou"

She told him of the entire story

Of all the deeds she had done

"All this was done for your glory

I have done all this for you my son-"

"Mother! How could you do this?

Have I ever wished for this land?

A king like Rama, this land should never miss

In his place, on his throne, I can never stand

Brother Rama is always above the rest

I am nothing but a servant to him

In this world, he is the very best

Without him, this land will remain grim

After my father's funeral, I will go

Go to the forest and beg him to return

If not, that exile I too shall undergo

If I ever take his place, I would rather burn"

The funeral lasted for eleven days and nights

The whole country mourned the death of their king

Of his father, Bharata performed the last rites

Such punishments onto them, God seemed to fling

After the funeral Bharata decided to go

He asked Sumantra to lead the way

Bharata, did all of Ayodhya follow

From Rama, they couldn't stay a second away

Bharata's chariot did Sumantra ride

His three mothers were coming behind

The entire kingdom was by their side

With the image of Rama, in everyone's mind

Ganga's bank, they reached soon
Guha saw them coming this way
They could see the pleasant rising moon
To welcome them Guha made no delay

Bharata then asked of where Rama was there
He asked if Guha could show them the way
But why he sought for Rama, Guha was unaware
Why did they need him, after sending him away?

Thus he asked, "O' Bharata, why are you here?
By finding Rama, what do you wish to do?
The reason for you to come, to me, is unclear
And you have brought an army along with you"

Bharata replied, "I am here to fix a mistake,
A grave mistake that my mother has made
The promise that she made I wish to break
Without Rama, Ayodhya will remain decayed

Rightfully, Rama should be the king

After my father, he is the father to me

Happiness back to Ayodhya, I wish to bring

A king, in all ways Rama is fit to be."

Guha was happy with Bharata's reply

The next day, his men Guha sent

"O' Bharata, for anything, on them, you can rely

Any trouble for you, they shall prevent"

To the Ashram did he then proceed

To receive them, Sage Bharadwaja was glad

Of hospitality he did every deed

He served them with everything he had

To the Maharshi, Bharata then said

"O' Prabhu, Rama is Ayodhya's rightful king

He is the only one who can take Kosala ahead

For this, him back to Ayodhya, I wish to bring

Please be kind enough to bless me,
Bless me by telling where he is right now
This is the only request I ask of thee
O' Prabhu, the only one who can help me is thou"

The sage gladly told him where to go
The very next day, Bharata then went
Where Rama is, they finally know
A moment without him, now couldn't be spent

Peaceful was the forest that day
Sita, Rama and Lakshmana were sitting there
Just then a rush of animals came their way
Of what was coming they were not aware

Rama said "O' Lakshmana, please climb a tree
Look for what is coming here
And tell me what is seen by thee
Tell me why these animals are running in fear"

As Rama said, he climbed up a tree
He saw Ayodhya's soldiers coming this way
In between, Bharata he could see
He could see them, rushing from miles away

"O' Rama, I can see Bharata from here
With all the soldiers, here, he came
He has come to kill us, that thing is clear
He came here to kill us, without any shame

Compared to us, that army is dust
Allow me to kill them, here and now
I shall even kill Bharata, if I really must
And for all that, I just need a word from thou"

"O' Lakshmana," Rama calmly said,
"Killing a person might prove you are brave
But apart from the land that turns red
All that is left is nothing but a grave

You brothers are everything to me
A kingdom, this way, I don't want to own
Even if I do, what is a kingdom without thee?
What is a kingdom, if it is just me alone?

And Bharata is someone I very well know
His own brothers, he has no intention to kill
He will never consider you or me as his foe
He will never think to harm us at his will

He would never go against you or me
Knowing him, he would have asked the king
To come here and take back, us three
Us back he would've sought to bring"

Lakshmana then realized his mistake
"O' Brother, I am sorry that I doubted him,
I am sure that our bond, he would never break
And doubting Bharata, for this was a mistake grim"

To that place did Bharata finally come
Sita, Rama and Lakshmana were living there
Looking at Rama, Bharata felt glum
Looking at that hut, he dwelled in despair

The fact that this was done for him
Was killing Bharata inside his wit
That Rama had to go through such a grim
Though for being the king only he was fit

Bharata went and touched Rama's feet
But Rama chose to hug him instead
Him, with a warm heart did Rama greet
And with a pleasant smile, he calmly said,

"O' Bharata, my blessings for you to be the king
An excellent king you should become
Always know and do the right thing
But O' Bharata, all the way here, why have you come?"

Bharata couldn't stop his tears
His eyes could no longer hide the pain
For the truth was painful and fierce
Yet, to Rama, the truth he had to explain

He told Rama of how Dasharatha died,
Rama felt the sorrow piercing his heart
Holding onto his hands, Bharata cried
He was heartbroken that his father had to depart

Without saying a word Rama sat there
While Sita in the corner, slowly wept
With blurry eyes, at the sky, did Lakshmana stare
But the truth at the end they had to accept

"O' Brother Rama", Bharata then said
"To become the king, only you are fit
Please become the king and take Ayodhya ahead
We are in need of you, your strength and wit

You will become the greatest king ever in time

Under you, Ayodhya shall be even more famed,

What my mother has done, is surely a crime

O' Rama, for what she has done, I am truly ashamed"

To Bharata, Rama calmly replied,

"O' Bharata, that isn't the case

Our mother's word shouldn't be denied

And our father's word, we cannot erase"

Bharata couldn't convince him, no matter what

Giving up, Bharata touched Rama's feet

"O' Rama, a king I shall become not

Although, on behalf of you, I shall hold that seat

To rule Ayodhya on your behalf, allow me

For fourteen years, of Ayodhya, I shall take care

For that, O' Rama, I shall take the sandals of thee

For, these sandals shall rule Ayodhya there

But, O' Rama, if you are not the king,
If you are not the king after fourteen years
Onto my life, I shall no longer cling
At that moment, my neck I shall pierce"

Bharata then placed those sandals on his head
And with deep sorrow Bharata took leave
Even among the people, the sorrow had spread
For leaving Rama, did they all grieve

Soon all the sages were moving away
Rama asked them their reason to go
They said, "Here, a demon has come to stay
And wherever he goes, does the darkness grow

Cruel, vicious and heartless is he
He can kill people with a single hand
O' Rama, he is the reason we have to flee
O' Rama, you should also go away from this land"

Sita, Rama and Lakshmana left that ground
They left that place, on the sage's advice
They left to Dandakaranya as the Sun crowned
And they walked and walked in the clear skies

They finally came to a level ground
To build their hut here, they decided
That place was peaceful with trees all around
For thirteen peaceful years there they resided

The three of them were chatting one day
Just then the demon Shurpanakha passed by
As her gaze fell on Rama, she couldn't take it away
For him, even God she was prepared to defy

She went to Rama and to him she told
"I am Shurpanakha, O' Handsome man
You seem to be so charming, strong and bold
Tell me who you are, as much as you can"

To Shurpanakha, who he is Rama calmly told
"O' Rama, I wish to marry thee", she said as a reply
"I always wanted to marry someone strong and bold,
I now know, no one is a match to the skills of thy"

Rama said, "O' Shurpanakha you must forgive me
For my Sita is already my wife,
And because of that I cannot marry thee
For Sita is the one I love with all my life

But my brother Lakshmana is there for you to wed
Like me he is also strong and bold"
"Oh yes, I could" that demon gleefully said
"Perhaps he is silver, if you are gold"

Towards Lakshmana she merrily ran
But he replied, "But Shurpanakha, as you can see
My skills are only second amongst the clan
Thus someone like me, is not meant for thee"

"Yes, Rama is the only one I can wed" she spoke

"But Rama, with that Sita I don't wish to share"

She jumped on, and Sita, she began to choke

Lakshmana severed her ears and nose then and there

Shurpanakha, screeching, ran away

Her shrieks made the birds fly high

And the scared animals ran in every way

Till the oceans you could hear her cry

Rivers, forests and oceans, she ran through

To the king, her brother, she then ran

To Lanka, screaming, she then rushed to

Lanka was ruled by Ravana and his clan

Her cries startled the people there

The animals ran away from that sound

She reached the palace on her feet bare

She ran to her brother stomping the ground

To her brother she then went and cried
Her screeches reached even the sky
Astounded were the courtiers beside
Even Ravana was astounded to see her cry

He looked at her and then said
"O' Dear, who is that, who did this to you
Whoever did this shall surely be dead
With their skin, your dress, I shall sew"

"O' Brother," Shurpanakha replied for that
"In the middle of the forest, two brothers stay
Their handsome looks I can keep staring at
The mighty king Dasharatha's sons are they

With them, a woman lives along
Sita happens to be her name
O' Brother, her beauty shines so strong
Her beauty makes the moon look lame

She is the reason this happened to me
She is the reason for my disgrace
O' Brother, I want you to destroy those three
Kill them and bring them to this place"

Angered Ravana came up with a way
He called the demon Maricha for that
"Maricha, my order you must obey
Only then, I can crush those three flat"

Who Rama was, Maricha knew
But to Ravana's orders he had to agree
Even though he did not want to
He agreed and left to search for those three

Rama's hut was filled with grace
With thousands of flowers around it
The birds and animals loved this place
There was beauty filled in every bit

Sita was playing with the birds
While the deer ran all around
For her, Ravana couldn't find words
To her beauty Ravana was bound

He ordered Maricha to turn into a golden deer
Maricha agreed and turned into one
In front of the hut did he then appear
And here and there he began to run

That beautiful deer Sita then saw
She went to Rama and then told
"O' Rama, that deer made me stare in awe
Can you bring me that deer made of gold?"

Rama replied, "O' Sita, I surely will
For I can never say no to thee
Your wish I shall surely fulfil
For fulfilling it is a pleasure to me

O' Lakshmana, with Sita, here you stay
While looking for that deer I shall go
Whatever happens never leave Sita away
Protect Sita at all costs, against any foe"

Behind that deer Rama then went
While Sita and Lakshmana stayed there
Rama went behind the deer Ravana sent
But of that fact he was not aware

Realizing that it was not a deer
Rama soon shot an arrow to kill it
Did Maricha's real form then appear
As by Rama's arrow, he got hit

Then in a desperate attempt to flee
In Rama's voice, Maricha then screeched
"O' Sita, O' Lakshmana! Help me!"
Sita and Lakshmana that voice then reached

Sita asked Lakshmana to help Rama there

Lakshmana then replied, "O' Devi, I cannot go

Until Rama comes, of your safety, I must take care

This is his order, and to his word I cannot say no"

Sita then said, "O' Lakshmana, listen to me

He might be in a problem, so grave

Thy brother needs the help of thee

Hence Rama you must go to and save"

Listening to Sita, Lakshmana replied

"O' Devi, to help Sri Rama I shall go

But the protection to you, I must provide

It shall protect you from any foe"

Then, around the hut Lakshmana drew a line

"O' Devi, to protect thee, this line I drew

Inside this line you are safe and fine

This line nobody can walk through

Whatever happens, please stay inside

No one can harm thee, whilst you are here

Whatever happens do not go outside

This line will not let anyone come near"

Saying so Lakshmana left, leaving Sita behind

Taking this chance did Ravana proceed

Dressed as a sage, wise and kind

He came to Sita as a sage in need

"Bhavati Bhiksham Dehi" did he say

"O' Lady, alms I ask from thee

Give me some food, O' Lady, I pray"

To Ravana's words, did Sita agree

She bought some food for him and told,

"O' Sage, this food please come and take"

Ravana replied, "O' Devi, I am very old

So please come here and give it, for my sake

"I am afraid I cannot come O' Sage

So please, I ask thee to come yourself"

Ravana replied, "Devi, you have set me in rage

How dare you order me to come myself?

Don't you know the traditions of your land

On your whole family curses shall fall

Unless you come and serve me with your hand

So now come, or my curse shall destroy you all"

At Sita, Ravana gleefully stared

She would surely come he had no doubt

Listening to him Sita was scared

So to give those alms, she then came out

Ravana shouted and laughed with glee

"Lady, you have fallen for my ploy

And in doing so, foolish was thee

By taking you away, Rama, I shall destroy"

Saying so he pulled her by her hair

While she was screaming he held her tight

And with his powers, he flew into the air

And while she was crying he took flight

"O' Rama! Purushottama! Save me!

Save me! O' Rama, my lord!"

Sita struggled to pull herself free

But then faster in the air, Ravana soared

The great vulture, Jatayu then heard Sita's cry

Of Dasharatha he was an old friend

To set her free, at once did he fly

For her, he was ready to fight till his end

He rushed towards that demon right away

Jatayu fought Ravana with all his might

Ravana fought like a creature gobbling his prey

Yet Jatayu gave his all in that fight

His sword, Ravana then took

And Jatayu's wing did he slash

Blood pouring out wherever they look

The mighty vulture fell in a flash

Looking at Jatayu, Sita felt grim

For, only for her, he came and fought

Sita deeply felt sorry for him

Sita cried for him and cried a lot

She then plucked the jewels she clad

And tied them all into a knot

These were now the only hope she had

The only hope that she could spot

She then dropped those jewels to the ground

In hope that someone would see

And would tell Rama, how they were found

So that Rama can come and set her free

Lanka, Ravana then took her to
Till then she did not stop her call
She called for Rama all the way through
Yet in that great distance her cry was small

To Sita, his kingdom Ravana showed
And boasted of himself all the day
Of how on Lanka gold had snowed
Of how every enemy he could slay

"Sita", he said, "why do you not want this?
All this luxury can belong to thee
With me, you can have all this bliss!
Hence forget that Rama and marry me"

"I might leave this world" Sita replied
"But my Rama, I can never leave
With Rama only, my life is tied
Without Rama, I can only grieve"

"But O' Lady, knots are meant to be broken
And this knot of yours I shall surely break
And a king can never break the words he has spoken
And for this word I shall put my life at stake

You belong to me and only me
For you to accept me I give you a year
After that I shall come and kill thee
I hope that I make myself very clear!"

He then went and told the demons there
"Very important for me is she
Of her every need you all take care
But whatever happens don't set her free

Ashokavan is a very nice place
You all may now take her there
Talk to her and tell her of its grace
But to go near her no man should dare"

Meanwhile, his brother did Lakshmana reach

"O' Rama, I was searching for you

From a distance I heard someone screech

For you I searched all the way through"

Rama said, "O' Lakshmana, that was not my plea

It was that deer-like demon's moan

I am fine, but Sita, where is she?

Lakshmana, why did you leave her alone?

To our hut, let us hurry back

About Sita, I am worried a lot

I am worried, ever since that last attack

It could be a demon's ploy, though I pray not"

They hurried back as soon as they could

Hurried only to see that Sita wasn't there

They searched and searched the whole wood

Where they found Jatayu with his breath so bare

He lay on the floor as his wing bled

He laid there, his face sorely paled

"I am sorry, O' Rama" Jatayu barely said

"I tried to save her, but I gravely failed"

"O' Jatayu, I can never blame you", Rama replied

"You have done so much, you tried your best"

While saying, his heart was breaking inside

Sita being away, Rama could not digest

"O' Rama, don't lose your heart

Your Sita you shall surely find"

Saying so did Jatayu depart

This whole world he had left behind

In Rama's eyes tears had dwelled

They soon rolled down his face

As Jatayu, in his hands, Rama held

Jatayu did Rama then embrace

Not only did he lose his wife

He had to see his dear friend die

He felt like this was the end of life

His heart felt empty and dry

"Lakshmana! I will destroy him

Whoever did this, their end is to come

He has put us into such a grim

For his sins he shall surely succumb"

Lakshmana replied, "O' Brother, calm down

What he has done is surely grave

And in his own sins, he shall drown

And Ma Sita we shall surely save

But for that, anger is not the way

'Analysis requires calm' you always said

'Do not let your heart go astray

Only then, in life can you move ahead'"

Rama then spoke, "O' Lakshmana, you are right,

For saving Sita, anger is not the way

Let us go and search for clues till night

Let us search for Sita all through the day"

On their way, they came across this one-eyed beast

For he only had two hands and an eye

With his bulky hands he would catch his feast

And devour them as they scream and cry

He saw Rama and Lakshmana coming his way

And as they came, he held them tight

He lifted them, ready to swallow his prey

But Lakshmana slit his hands with effort so slight

Rama shot an arrow into the giant's eye

In an instant the beast lost his hold

And with pain he let out a screeching cry

And after a moment, he turned cold

Out of him a Gandharva came
And said, "O' Rama, Lakshmana, thank you
Because of you, myself I became
My curse you both overthrew

A Gandharva I am, and Kabandha is my name
All I can give you, for helping me,
Is the knowledge needed to reach your aim,
This is where you can find what is required to thee

In Kishkindha there is a mountain
You will find the monkey king Sugriva there
You going there shall not be in vain
You will find there, solutions, to your despair"

Saying so, did Kabandha disappear
Following his word did Rama and Lakshmana leave
What they would find there was still unclear
But for finding Sita, some clues they might achieve

An old lady they met on their way

She was waiting for Rama to arrive

"Sri Rama, welcome! "Did Shabari say

"Just to see you, so much did I strive"

Shabari was Rama's deep devotee

In her life all she wanted was to see him

"O' Prabhu, thank you for coming to see me

My life has been brightened and shall never get dim

To me, you have come all the way

For you to eat, these berries I have got"

Serving them to Rama, did she pray

She served them in some twines tied in a knot

"O' Shabari, thank you" Rama smiled and replied

But Shabari cut in, as he picked the berries few

"O' Rama, the berries might be sour inside!

Can I taste them before giving them to you?"

As he agreed, from each berry she took a bite

And to Rama, she only gave the ones sweet

"O' Rama", Lakshmana spoke, "to eat these is it right,

After she tasted them, are they good for you to eat?"

~

"When with such love she is giving them to me,

O' Lakshmana, them, how can I not take?

To such devotion, how can I disagree?

If I refuse them, it is surely a mistake"

~

Those berries with bliss, Rama then had

"O' Shabari, these berries are the sweetest of all,

For eating these berries I am very glad

For me the devotion matters no matter how small"

~

He then blessed Shabari, and took leave from there

Rama and Lakshmana, for Kishkindha they went

For still, what was to come they were unaware

Yet they went with finding Sita as their sore intent

~

In Kishkindha there was a hill

There lived Sugriva, the monkey king

Down, he saw two men walking uphill

Also weapons with them, they seemed to bring

His minister Hanuman, he then asked to come

"O' Hanuman, do you see those men two?

Go, check who they are, and where they are from

And why did they decide to walk this hill through?

I doubt if they were sent by the brother mine

To kill me, he sent them is what I doubt

If you see them crossing any line

Within a second, you send them out

Rather than stopping them suddenly, instead

Turn into a Brahmin and then, them you stop"

Hanuman turned into a Brahmin as the king said

And jumped down the mountain in a single hop

Obeying the king did Hanuman then go

He went and stopped those men there

He asked, "O' Sir, who may you be, may I know?

Who are you and you have come from where?"

"I am Rama" that young man said

"And I am Lakshmana" the other replied

"Towards king Sugriva we both are to head

Someone told that help to us, he might provide"

Of Rama, Hanuman was a great devotee

So who Rama was Hanuman knew

He then returned to his form of a monkey

And warmly greeted those men two

"O' Prabhu, my king is the one you are looking for

I am Hanuman, the minister of the monkeys

I shall not obstruct your path anymore

I shall follow you, however you please

I shall take you there if you permit

King Sugriva I can take you to

I shall take you there if you allow it

I am sure he would be pleased to meet you"

Hanuman jumped up the hill as they agreed

And to them he began to show the way

Towards King Sugriva did he then lead

He led them to where the king was to stay

Them, with warmth did king Sugriva greet

Rama then told him why they came

"O' Sugriva, you, Kabandha told us to meet

He told us to find the king, Sugriva by name"

To Sugriva, about Sita, Rama then told

Of what happened Rama told him about

He asked if there are any clues he might hold

He asked if Sugriva could help them out

"Sri Rama, we can help" Sugriva then said
"A lady's screams we heard, few days ago
'Rama, Purushottama' cried the voiceover overhead
And this pile of jewels did the woman throw

O' Rama tell me, if to Devi Sita, they belong"
But Lakshmana replied as soon as he saw
"These anklets Ma Sita was wearing all along
I can tell they belong to her without a flaw

When I prayed to her feet everyday
I noticed, on them these anklets she had
Therefore without a doubt I can say
These are the anklets that Ma Sita clad"

Those jewels Rama held in his hand
In them his Sita seemed to appear
All that sorrow he could not withstand
He so wished that she was near

"O' Rama, I feel your pain" Sugriva said
"My wife has been taken by the brother mine
By my own brother Vali, who has been misled
For, without this mistake all would have been fine"

To Rama, Sugriva explained his past,
How he and Vali were so dear to each other
Though this kinship was not long to last,
For Sugriva became an enemy of his brother

The kingdom of Kishkindha, Vali ruled, long ago
He ruled over this land full of peace
The fun in this kingdom only seemed to grow
The joy in these monkeys never seemed to cease

There lived a demon, Mayavi by the name
With his mighty body, he looked like a beast
One day to Kishkindha, this demon came
And on anyone he saw there, he would feast

He came and challenged the king alone
And for his people, the king Vali agreed
In a blink, Mayavi was lifted and thrown
Terrified Mayavi, into a cave he scurried

Vali alone went into that cave
He told Sugriva to wait outside
Sugriva thought Vali was enough brave
Yet horrible screeches came from inside

Sugriva waited, waited and waited there
Yet for a long time Vali did not come
Slowly he was engulfed in despair
Yet he prayed that his brother did not succumb

Blood came oozing from the cave after a bit
The blood oozing out was a bright red
With a heavy heart, Sugriva looked at it
Sugriva thought that Vali was dead

He was fully taken over by fear

With his only hope, he took a huge rock

Towards the cave he rolled that sphere

And that whole cave with it did he block

He returned to Kishkindha clenching his heart

All that happened to his people did he unfold

People told him that his kingship he should start

Sugriva became the king as the people told

Vali however was not dead

He killed the demon in his fight

It was the demon's blood, oozing red

He killed Mayavi with all his might

While returning he noticed the huge rock

He wondered who could have done that

After he returned Vali had his shock

That on his throne Sugriva sat

Vali's blood boiled at what Sugriva had done
Him, his own brother seemed to betray
All this time they both have been one
He never thought he would see such a day

To Vali, Sugriva tried to calmly explain,
Vali was engulfed by his anger own
Vali's anger was clogging his own brain
All that anger on Sugriva he had shown

Kishkindha, Vali told Sugriva to leave
And from Sugriva, his wife Ruma did he take
Because of this, did Sugriva grieve and grieve
Those brothers were separated by this mistake

Thus Sugriva lives on this hill
To live, Rishyamuka, was the only place
The only place where Vali couldn't come and kill
This is the only land to avoid Vali's chase

"O' Rama", Sugriva finally said

"To help each other, a pact, let us make

Kill Vali, and of Kishkindha, make me the head

And I will ask my army to search for Lady Sita's sake"

Rama then thought about this plan

And decided to help Sugriva out

For the attack on Vali, preparations began

Sugriva was to win without a doubt

Rama told Sugriva to challenge his kin

And as Rama told, Sugriva did

Very soon did the brothers' fight begin

Meanwhile on a tree, Rama quietly hid

While they were fighting, Rama looked for a turn

In a split second Vali he could kill

With his arrow on the bow, he sat stern

He could never miss Vali with his skill

Sugriva and Vali were fighting strong
They fought with trees, stones, fists and feet
They both fought and fought for so long
To distinguish between them was a difficult feat

Then, an idea, Hanuman got
A garland of flowers on Sugriva he set
Then who Vali was, Rama could spot
Then Rama shot at Vali without a fret

Vali, did that arrow go and hit
Wounded he fell on to the ground
Beside Vali did Sugriva sit
Sugriva felt sad, so did all around

"O' Brother", to Vali, he quietly said,
"For your mistake, I had to kill you
Kishkindha you could have happily led
If what had happened you truly knew

Yet with anger you seemed to go blind
And with it you banished the brother of thee
If only to listen you were enough kind
Such a day, we would never have to see"

Vali then understood what he had done
And that what he had done was a mistake grave
And that his actions benefited none
And of his foolishness he had become a slave

He then said, "O' Brother, I hope you forgive me
You are my brother, no matter what
And I shouldn't have behaved such with thee
Destiny, at least now, us together it has brought

Please take care of Tara my wife
And also look after Angada my son
Here, an end shall come to my life
Bur for you, as the king it had just begun

By the arrow of Lord Rama, I am happy to die

I am happy to die, with enemies none

I am happy to die looking at the sky

I am happy, that in this fight you have won"

Saying so Vali passed away

He had passed with his brother beside

For Vali, then did Sugriva pray

And consoled Tara, who bitterly cried

"Angada shall be the crowned prince" Sugriva said

He decided that him, Angada would succeed

Then of Kishkindha Sugriva became the head

He became one of the best kings of Kishkindha indeed

For a long time, as the king did he enjoy

He enjoyed himself, he enjoyed a lot

As the king, he had had all the joy

So much, that his promise to Rama, he forgot

Meanwhile Rama thought that their word was broken

He felt that to his word Sugriva did not abide

As for such a long time, Sugriva hasn't spoken

Rama felt grief swelling from inside

Sita, for such a long time he did not see,

To find her, Rama did not know where to go

He didn't know how to set her free

Of how she is, he did not know

Looking at Rama, Lakshmana was blue

Looking at Rama, even Hanuman couldn't hold

To go and tell Sugriva, decided the two

That his promise as a king, he must uphold

They both walked up to the king

Sugriva was enjoying himself there

Lakshmana could not hold a thing

Looking at Sugriva, he just couldn't bear

Angered, he then shouted and told
"Sugriva, what you have done is not right
Your promise you have failed to withhold
Yet, you, here, seem so cheery and bright

The word that he gave, my brother fulfilled it
Because of him, you are the king right now
Because of him, on that throne you can sit
Yet so easily you have broken your vow"

Sugriva, then did Hanuman remind
"O' Sugriva, don't forget the word you gave
You promised Sri Rama, that Ma Sita you will find
You promised him, that Ma Sita you will save

As a king, your word, you must not break
As, to the people, you will become an example bad
One should never run from the words they make
For it destroys the trust the people had had"

Because of Rama, his life as a king had begun

And to him, Rama's help was severe

Sugriva then realized the mistake that he had done

This mistake was one, he had to clear

To Rama, he then went, and forgiveness did he ask

He then summoned his army to come as one

And all of them were given a single task

The search for Sita had then begun

The army was divided into groups four

To them his royal marks Rama gave

Holding onto them, for Sita, they were to explore

All the monkeys in there, were strong and brave

The southern group did Hanuman lead

King Jambavan was a part of it also

For Rama, Hanuman was ready to do any deed

And utmost devotion to Rama did he show

Hanuman, did Rama then kindly bless

And said, "O' Hanuman, when to the south you go

And if in finding Sita, you find success

This royal ring of mine to her you show"

Then at Sugriva's word did all of them leave

They left as soon as Sugriva said

In finding Sita, did they surely believe

Then to the Southern coast did Hanuman head

Searching for Sita, far south did they reach

They were searching for Sita everywhere

Searching for her they came to a beach

After not finding her they felt a bit of despair

Then they saw a vulture overhead

Who he was, Jambavan knew

"Is this Sampati?" Jambavan said

"We knew your brother and thus know you"

To them then Sampati came
"So you know the dear brother mine
No wonder you thus know my name
How is my brother? I hope he is fine"

Jambavan said, "I am afraid; you never got to know,
Your brother, right now, in heaven he is
But while dying, so much bravery did he show
No one can pay for the sacrifice of his"

Listening to him, Sampati felt sad,
"Who killed the brother of mine?
Against my brother what venom they had?
Who was it, who had such spine?"

Jambavan then sadly replied,
"O' Sampati, Ravana is his name
To protect Ma Sita from him, Jatayu tried
For your brother's death, he is to blame"

"The name Ravana did I just hear?

If I knew that my brother he would kill

To this land, I wouldn't have let him come near

I would have tried to stop him with all my skill"

Angada then said, "You have seen Ravana, you say?"

Could you tell us where he could be?

To him, could you show us the way?

If you can, we will all be grateful to thee"

Sampati replied, "Oh yes, I can surely help you

Ravana is in that island far, far away

But for that you have to cross that ocean through

As to go to Lanka, that is the only way"

Sampati replied

"Thank you O' Sampati" Angada then said,

"You have done us a favor we can never repay

Now towards Lanka, to Ma Sita we can head

But who can cross this mighty ocean all the way?"

Then Jambavan said, "I surely could,

If I were young, I could have done it

But now I am old and my powers are not as good

Thus I cannot do it, I must admit

But among us there is one who can

He is the only one who can cross that sea

With such power there is only one man

O' Hanuman, it is none other than thee"

Hanuman then said, "O' Jambavan, how can I?

The powers you speak of, I have none

I do not understand the words of thy

To cross the ocean, I surely am not the suitable one"

At Hanuman then did Jambavan smile

"O' Hanuman, about your powers, you forgot

You have got so many abilities in a pile

Such that a weakness in you, no one can spot

When you were young you had a curse on you

That your own abilities you will forget

Until one tells thee about your powers true

Thus your story to you, I now shall set

To Anjana and Pavana you were born

You were loved deeply by them both

Both of their lives did you adorn

They were so contented watching your growth

One day, when the sunrise had just begun

You mistook the red sun for a fruit

You then started flying towards the Sun

You went out of the earth on your route

The whole Sun, you tried to eat

But you couldn't eat something so hot

As you couldn't defeat the Sun's heat

That swollen jaw of yours, you got

Injured, you then fell to the ground

Such a bad bruise on your jaw, you had

That when, about you, Pavana found,

For you, Hanuman, he felt so sad

With anger, the air did he erase

With this, the world was set in despair

No one could breathe in any place

To survive, they had to reduce his flare

Pavana did all the Gods then plea

Yet his reaction remained the same

He told them he was very sad about thee

Listening to him, to you, they all came

You, the Lord of Gods Indra said to

'O' Hanuman, to you this is a boon of mine

The weapons of Gods shall never touch you

They shall have no effect on this body thine'

Then the God of fire, Agni said

'O' Hanuman, you cannot be harmed by flame

You cannot be harmed by the fire red

Any amount of fire, you can easily tame'

Then did the creator Brahma state,

'My Asthra, to affect you, it shall cease

You can also now lift any weight

You can also change your form as you please

Also a powerful immortal I shall make you

There shall never come a time when you die

There shall be nothing that you cannot do

Hanuman, you shall live forever, hereby'

The Sun God Surya, then told

'O' Hanuman, I am sorry to hurt thee

You with knowledge I shall mould

I shall give you all the wisdom I have with me'

To you many boons, gave the Gods all

So many boons they gave each

They gave you gains, big and small

With such powers, anything you could reach

With this Pavana was happy again

Thus, that curse did he then lift

All the air flowed into the world then

Into this world, the air did he shift

Even with all these powers you have got,

At the end, you were still a child

With such powers, you could never get caught

With that mischief of yours, you went wild

One day, while playing, you saw a sage wise

You tried to annoy him for the fun of it

But whatever you did, he did not open his eyes

For a long time there did he silently sit

After a while, he was angered by you

Thus he said, "You had the nerve to disturb me

You shall forget your powers, your whole life through

Until someone reminds you about the powers of thee"

Yet as the God Surya, his word he kept

The Sun God, Guru to you he had become

And as his disciple, you did he accept

The Sun is where you got your knowledge from

Along with him, you roamed the earth round

Along with him, the world, did you learn

You, with wisdom, did he surround

And like that, into a man, did you turn

O' Hanuman, your story to you, now I have told

To you, your past did I remind

Now you know of the powers you hold

You know that you are one of a kind

Go to Lanka by crossing the sea

Go to Lanka by crossing this wave

Go and there Ma Sita you see

And give her the ring Sri Rama gave"

About his powers Hanuman got to know

He then knew exactly what to do

Into the size of a mountain did he grow

He seemed to touch the sky as he grew

In the sand, a valley, he seemed to create

Then did Hanuman look at the ground

It looked like it couldn't hold his weight

For a stronger land he looked around

Then he found Mahendra Giri beside

His weight, that hill seemed to bear

And to fit his feet it was enough wide

He climbed it, and for flight did he prepare

Then in a jump, he took his flight

The jump made a sound so loud

That the animals ran around in fright

And of the dust it made a huge cloud

He then flew along with the air

With the birds, he flew along

Far away, Lanka, he could see from there

He knew it would take him, a journey so long

Down below he saw the sea

And then looked up at the sky

It was a deep blue wherever you see

In such a scene, it was a pleasure to fly

But he knew he had no time for fun

Sri Rama's orders he must fulfil

And he cannot rest until it's done

For this he must use all his skill

Hanuman was noticed by the God of the sea

Then mount Mynaka did Sea God Samudra call

Then he said, "O' Mynaka, I have an order for thee

For Hanuman, do this favor small

Hanuman, for Rama, is doing his best

But I can tell that he must be tired

So go and on you, let him rest

As for doing this much work, rest is required"

Upon telling, did the mountain Mynaka go,

Mynaka was a mountain who lived in the sea

Then up to the sea surface did he grow

He grew tall enough for Hanuman to see

And then said, "O' Hanuman, I know you,

Your father Vayu, is a friend of mine

For crossing this sea, I acknowledge your valor true

In this world, your resolve is sure to shine

But I feel like you seem to need a break

Why don't you come and rest on me?

My hospitality you please come and take

I shall be very pleased to help thee"

Hanuman then replied, "O' Mynaka, I thank you

But at this moment I cannot stop

What Sri Rama told, I have to do

Sri Rama's orders I cannot drop"

Him, Mynaka tried hard to persuade

But on his word, Hanuman stood still

Whatever happened, on his word he stayed

No matter what, he stuck to Sri Rama's will

But because of this he could not go ahead

To go ahead, Mynaka did not let

But quickly to Lanka he had to head

But for that past Mynaka he has to get

Then on Mynaka's peak did he pat
And said, "O' Mynaka, think like this
Think that on your peak I just sat
Your hospitality now, I did not miss"

Then Mynaka accepted and said,
"O' Hanuman, your devotion has awed me
This devotion of yours, it shall spread
May you be successful in whatever is done by thee"

Thus after taking his blessings, Hanuman went
Over the calm and mighty ocean did he fly
Flying over the blue, every second he spent
With devotion, he didn't blink an eye

Then after a while he encountered a snake
She broke out of the water, and as she did
Such a loud splash out of it did she make
It created a whirlpool where she stood amid

"I am Surasa" she hissed and said,
"I now have a wish to eat you
And so I will not let you move ahead
Until thee, I now blissfully chew"

Hanuman then said, "O Surasa, I cannot,
I cannot let myself be eaten by thee
For an order from Sri Rama, I have got
This really isn't the time to eat me"

In protest, bigger did Surasa grow
Hanuman was now so easy to eat
But to grow Hanuman wasn't slow
He grew so tall, he left her at his feet

But even Surasa was not holding back
Taller than Hanuman she then grew
But in wit, Hanuman did not lack
He grew taller before Surasa knew

Like that they grew taller and taller

To lose this fight neither had the will

They grew so much that the ocean seemed smaller

But no matter what, they were equal in skill

At last did Surasa laugh and hiss

"Hanuman, choice you now have none

Going into my mouth you cannot miss

As from here you can never run"

Then Hanuman used his wit

Into the size of an ant did he shrink

And went into her mouth and came out of it

He did all this in one of Surasa's blink

Then he came to his size and then told

"O' Surasa, into your mouth did I just go

Me you no longer have the right to hold

For, to what I have done, you cannot say no"

Surasa was pleased with Hanuman's wit

She came to her form of a girl and said,

"O' Hanuman, you are second to none, I must admit

I was just testing you, for the power of your head

I was sent by Lord Brahma to test thee

You, for your wit, I was sent to test

You have truly astounded me

You, in your kind, are surely the best"

Then for Hanuman she left the way,

And then Hanuman went ahead

He hoped to reach without delay

Thus towards Lanka did he hurriedly head

But on the way, a demon stood

Cruel she was, and Simhika was her name

By her look, you know, she was up to no good

And with that look towards him she came

Of Lanka, she was the guardian at the sea
"You have no place here" she cruelly said
"To go past here you are not allowed by me
Thus in an instant, you shall be dead"

Towards Hanuman did she then descend
Towards Hanuman she seemed to drag her feet
And over him, her mouth did she extend
And the whole of him at once did she eat

Into her mouth, Hanuman went
And into her stomach, he had to go
But being eaten here he had to prevent
Thus into an enormous size did he grow

He grew taller and taller by every flash
He grew bigger than what she could resist
And thus her stomach did he slash
Soon did Simhika seize to exist

At the far end, Hanuman saw a beach

For hiding he turned to the size of a cat

Finally, Lanka did he soon reach

He flew so far to achieve just that

He stepped on to the land and sneaked into it

He made sure no one saw him there

He cleverly escaped the guards bit by bit

He silently escaped those demons' glare

But at the end Hanuman was noticed by one

His coming did Lanka's Shakti Lankini sense

Without her notice, who can enter Lanka are none

And thus, Ravana appointed her for the gate's defense

Lankini was the demon Goddess of this island

Without her word, to Lanka, no one can come

If they do, as soon as they step on her land

In her hands they are sure to succumb

She went and stopped Hanuman on his way

And said, "You thought I couldn't see you here?

From my sight you cannot get away

To this land of mine, you cannot come near"

Hanuman came to his size and respectfully said,

"O' Great Shakti, why I am here, I am sure you know

Therefore towards Ma Sita I must head

And for that, to your land, please let me go"

Whatever he said she did not agree

She did not let Hanuman to go on with his quest

Since no matter what, she did not let him free

Hanuman's patience she seemed to test

Hanuman lost his patience at last

Thus, Lankini, on the stomach he hit

Lankini fell on to the floor completely aghast

And as she realized her teeth did she grit

Lord Brahma once told her long ago

That if, because of a monkey, she ever fell,

Lanka will then meet its strongest foe

And in its downfall, Lanka shall dwell

She then said, "O' Hanuman, forgive me

I have now realized who thee is true

I now have no work left with thee

For, destruction of Lanka begins with you

And for this, I cannot do anything

For no matter what, Lanka shall end

Though to me, this truth will sting,

But future isn't a thing that I can mend"

Those words to Hanuman did she say

Then, leaving Hanuman, she left from there

Then into Lanka, Hanuman went his way

For Sita he tried searching everywhere

For Sita, Hanuman looked around

Lanka was a place so beautifully green

Heaven, here, seemed to come to the ground

Its beauty was one, never before seen

Every corner of it, shone like gold

Every inch of it was filled with bliss

The beauty of it could not be told

But the eyes thrive to see a sight like this

Hanuman looked for Sita here and there

He searched for her, left and right

He searched here, there and everywhere

He looked for her with all his might

To search further, to the palace he went

He found a lady, sleeping in a room

Seeing her, he knew, what beauty had meant

Her face like a flower, it seemed to bloom

Mandodari was what she was called

She was the wife of Ravana, the king

Of her beauty everyone was enthralled

From heaven, herself, she seemed to bring

Hanuman thought, "Ma Sita, she must be,

She is the only one to be as beautiful as this

But she seems to be so full of glee,

Ma Sita would definitely not be at bliss

So lavishly, Ma Sita wouldn't have slept,

If from Sri Rama, she was this away

She would have struggled and cried and wept

She would have cried and wept all the way"

Then Hanuman left that place

But his search did not cease

To every corner did he then race

But he couldn't find her in any of these

With this failure, he could not cope
Sri Rama's order he could not do
With this, Hanuman lost all hope
This bitter truth he could not walk through

He thought, "Like this Sri Rama, I cannot face,
My Lord's order I failed to fulfil
But without fulfilling I cannot leave this place
Better than this, myself, I shall kill

But there is one place I did not see
To Ashokavan I am yet to go
That is where Ma Sita must be
Once I go there, I shall get to know"

With flickering hope he flew till there
Down, a woman was sitting under a tree
That woman seemed so kind and fair
She is Sita, she surely must be

Towards her, did he come and stop

By this time, it was already night

Hanuman placed himself on the tree top

He wished not to startle her by his sight

Then towards her a man then came

That man was so handsome and tall

In front of him, anyone was lame

In front of him, everyone seemed small

He seemed to shine, in that dark night

With his charm, he seemed to glow

In this darkness, only he was bright

Compared to him the moon seemed low

He came to Sita and harshly said

"Sita, my promised time is to come to an end

If you don't accept me, I shall see you dead,

Whether you live or not, on your word it shall depend"

Sita then plucked a grass blade beside

Showed it to Ravana and then said,

"You are this when my Rama is by my side,

Than to be with you, I am better to be dead

My Rama, is forever, the king of mine

If Rama is a temple, you are a grave

You are not even a flicker compared to his shine

For, my Rama is the king and you are a slave"

Angered, Ravana left her there

His slaves came to where Sita sat

They came to her with an angry glare

Her, they told Ravana was angry at

They tried to convince her to marry their king

They told her of Ravana's grace

But, Sita did not accept a thing

In her heart, Rama, no one could replace

Yet to convince her they tried and tried,

Then to shoo those slaves a demoness came

She then came and stood by Sita's side

That demoness was called Trijata by name

Then to the slaves did she say

"Go away and leave Sita in my care

At least now, peacefully, let her stay

To touch her now, nobody should dare

Ravana's downfall we cannot defy

For I had a dream just about this

That in Sri Rama's hands, Ravana shall die

And about this dream there is nothing amiss

Rama is said to be the most powerful one

And Sita is said to be his love true

In this whole world, he is second to none

Our king is nothing compared to his hue"

Listening to Trijata, did the slaves leave,

Shortly even Trijata left, to go and sleep

Sitting under the tree did Sita then grieve

Sitting below the tree, did she gently weep

All the memories of Rama, surrounded her

Those beautiful moments with Rama she had

Together with each, so happy they were

Just thinking of them, made Sita so sad

Hanuman was watching her from above the tree,

Down, he saw, Ma Sita started to cry

Ma Sita, like that, he could not see

To reduce her glum, Hanuman had to try

But if he jumps down in a single move

Ma Sita he would surely scare,

But from her, that sorrow he had to remove

For he could not see her crying there

Then an excellent idea Hanuman got,

Rama's story from there did he sing

That song, Sita's attention it caught

For it was a song about Sita's king

Rama's story to Sita he told

Rama's tale, Hanuman sang from above

Sita's grieving heart that song consoled

Sita's heart lightened with Rama's love

That song felt like warm Sunlight

And as that song went through her ear

Sita felt her heart feeling bright

She felt as though her Rama was near

Hanuman dropped Rama's ring from there

That ring went, and on Sita's lap it fell

Sita held that ring with utmost care

That ring fell to her as if by a spell

She knew that it was Rama's ring,

She felt like she was in a dream

For that ring, here, who would bring

For who could have done a work so extreme

Holding the ring did Sita stand

She was listening to that song so sweet

Then Hanuman came down to the land

Smiling, he then touched Sita's feet

He said, "To Sri Rama, a servant am I

O' Janani, Hanuman is what they call me

To any distance for you I can fly

Thus I was sent by Sri Rama to rescue thee

In Rama's hands, is Ravana's death

But till then you don't have to stay here

I can take you to Sri Rama in a single breath

With me as your servant, you have nothing to fear"

Looking at Hanuman Sita then told with a smile,
"O' Hanuman, thank you for coming for me
For me you have crossed so many a mile
But I am sorry for I cannot come with thee

O' Hanuman, I cannot come with you
For to Sri Rama I have tied the thread
Me, from here, only he can rescue
Thus, leave me here and go ahead"

Hanuman then said, "O' Janani, to you I am a son
A mother can surely come with her lad
Thus, I see, there is a problem none
O' Janani, there is no need for you to remain sad"

Sita smiled and said, "O' Hanuman, that is true
But there are so many captured apart from me
Leaving them captured, I cannot come with you
Only if Ravana dies, will they truly be free

And only by Rama, will Ravana die,

Therefore, Sri Rama has to come here

Then Ravana's death even God cannot deny

That will be end of these captives' fear

O' Hanuman, I have a favor for you

I shall now give this gemstone to thee

Sri Rama, go and give this Chintamani to

For, this will show him that you have met me"

Kneeling at her feet, did Hanuman reply

"O' Janani, your word I truly regard

There is no end, for this kindness thy

For justice, you endure, no matter how hard

Thus, here, I shall take leave of you

Sri Rama is sure to come for thee

You are sure to see Ravana's death through

Sri Rama will surely set these captives free"

"O' Hanuman", then Sita kindly said,

"You came across the ocean without a break

There is a garden of fruits, just ahead

The fruits on those trees, you can take"

Listening to Sita, did Hanuman agree,

For he was now feeling hungry as well

For without a break he had crossed the sea

Now into his stomach's desire he had to dwell

He took off to the sky, after touching her feet

When he saw this garden, did he then land

Then every fruit in that place did he eat

He ate everything he could touch with his hand

While eating he was filled with joy,

He started jumping and playing everywhere

Like that, the whole garden, did he destroy

He enjoyed himself without a care

Hanuman was spotted by the troops of the king

Towards Hanuman did the soldiers run

But to Hanuman's might, they were not a thing

With them, Hanuman just had some fun

He thought, "With these demons we will have to fight

With them, we will be at war anyway

Then before going back, I should see their might

For that, with these demons, I now can play"

Towards Hanuman did the soldiers rush,

Hanuman, they thought they could defeat

All of their hopes did Hanuman crush

All to a pulp, did Hanuman beat

To Hanuman's might they were so small

Still towards him, did they all race

Hanuman simply thrashed them all

He hit them all with his giant mace

Then, to Hanuman, went Ravana's youngest son

To fight with Hanuman did he go

But within a second Hanuman had won

Him, onto a chariot did Hanuman throw

Then Ravana's eldest son went to avenge his kin

Indrajit went and challenged Hanuman outright

Soon between them, did the fight begin

Amongst everyone, Indrajit gave the toughest fight

He then used the Brahmastra against his foe

Indrajit's victory, had to be sure with this

Towards Hanuman did the Brahmastra go

And hitting Hanuman, it did not miss

But on Hanuman, it would have an effect none

As Lord Brahma's boon, Hanuman had

To Hanuman, there was no harm done

Around him the Brahmastra just gracefully clad

Yet Hanuman just stood over there,

To Lord Brahma he must show his regard

Over there, he hence stood square

Around him, the Brahmastra formed a guard

He then thought, "Now, with them I cannot fight,

For Lord Brahma's Astra I don't wish to break

I anyway should know Ravana's might

So I will let myself be captured, for that sake"

"That monkey finally lost to someone" they thought

To defeat Hanuman, so many have tried

Hanuman, now they finally caught

Hanuman, with ropes, they quickly tied

Hanuman, to Ravana, did they then take

In the middle of the hall they made him stand

Indrajit said, "O' Father, he made a big mistake

This monkey dared to step into this palace land

Our beautiful gardens did he deface

He killed my brother on top of it

He smashed everything with his mace

Unforgivable sins did this monkey commit"

To Hanuman, then Ravana angrily said

"To step on my land how can you dare?

In my place, such havoc you have spread

And you still stand here, without a care"

To Ravana, then, Hanuman replied,

"To respect a messenger, is this the way?

You have brought me here, crudely tied

And without offering a seat, you just let me stay?"

His ropes did he then easily break

And extended his long long tail

With it, a throne for himself did he make

In front of his throne, Ravana's looked pale

Hanuman then sat on top of that throne

And said, "Hanuman is what you can call me

As the minister of Sugriva, I am known

To give a message of Sri Rama, I have come to thee

Capturing Ma Sita was surely a sin

Thus, to Sri Rama, let Ma Sita go

If not, a deadly war is to begin

And you shall be dead, before you know"

Angered Ravana ordered to kill,

"You have chosen to come yourself to death

I should let Sita free? I never will

And for asking, you shall take your last breath"

Then in the court did Vibhishana stand

And said, "O' Brother, this is not right

You shouldn't kill a messenger, who came to your land

With a messenger you should never fight"

About Vibhishana, then Hanuman thought,

"To Ravana, he seems to be a kin

Yet to Ravana, about Dharma he taught

He seems to have wisdom about virtue and sin"

Ravana then said, "Foolish brother, as if I care

For it's my order to fire this monkey's tail

I want to see his throne, set aflare

And I shall laugh as he grows pale and pale"

On Hanuman's tail, flames were lit

But Hanuman didn't feel even a bit of pain

Hanuman did not feel even a bit of it

All of Ravana's moves were set in vain

Yet in pain, Hanuman seemed to yell

He acted to be in pain, and stomped the ground

The fact that he was acting, no one could tell

Hanuman screeched and started to jump around

Like that with fire, the court did he fill,
The whole court, with his tail, he lit
And then he jumped out of the window sill
He started to burn all of Lanka, bit by bit

He swished his tail round and round
And all around the kingdom did he race
Like that he set fire all around
As he jumped from place to place

Fire was set to the city entire
So quickly did the fire spread
The whole land was set on fire
The whole land was glowing red

After all this, Hanuman thought
"Such a foolish thing, I just did
What if, in this fire, Ma Sita just got caught?
I was just having fun, acting like a kid"

To Ashokavan he soon went
To see if Ma Sita was fine
To Ashokavan there wasn't a dent
It was as peaceful as a shrine

The Ashokavan that fire did not harm
The fire did not harm this one place
It was protected, as if by a charm
Ashokavan remained peaceful, filled with grace

Sita again did Hanuman meet,
He checked if she was alright
And then prayed to Sita's feet
And left Lanka in the dead of night

By now they two were like a mother and her lad
She considered Hanuman to be her son
For he brightened the only hope she ever had
In that darkness he came like the ray of sun

Hanuman excitedly flew across the sea,

To Sri Rama, he wanted to tell everything,

He wanted to tell everything that he did see

He couldn't imagine the joy it would bring

Soon Hanuman then reached the shore

On Mahendra Giri did he then land

He told his group of all that happened before

That joy they all could not withstand

Jumping and laughing, they all ran back,

To Kishkindha they all started to head

They laughed and jumped all through the track

Singing and dancing they all moved ahead

They reached Madhuvan on their way

Of that garden, Dadhimukha took care

Over there to rest, did Hanuman's team stay

They decided to take a break and rest there

Dadhimukha who took care of this ground

To Vali and Sugriva, an uncle was he

Thus Hanuman and his team could stay around

To do anything here, they were totally free

They hopped and jumped here and there

They jumped and destroyed the land

They caused such havoc everywhere

Seeing them destroying, Dadhimukha couldn't stand

To Sugriva, Dadhimukha then ran

To him about Hanuman and his team he told

Of how the havoc in Madhuvan began

Of how they destroyed this garden of gold

To his surprise, Sugriva's face was lit

He seemed happier than ever before

But how could Sugriva be happy at it!

Such bitter news how can he adore!

"Such good news to me you brought
You have pulled me out of such blue
O' Dadhimukha, worry not
For I will have it rebuilt for you"

Confused Dadhimukha asked the king,
"O' King, I did not follow the words of thee
How can we be happy of such a thing?
What is the reason, could you please tell me?"

"O' Dadhimukha, if Hanuman's team were sad,
They wouldn't dare to dance in joy
That means some sort of good news they had
Which forced them to dance, sing and destroy

Most likely, Devi Sita, they have seen,
Thus to return here, they were all glad
If they didn't see her, this couldn't be the scene
If they didn't see her, they would all be sad"

Just then Hanuman's group came into the hall

Like stars did all their faces glow

So happy and cheerful were they all

Their happiness only seemed to grow

Of all that happened Hanuman told

Sugriva felt so happy with this

His heart was bright and shining like gold

All of them were dwelling in bliss

Then they noticed Dadhimukha there

All of a sudden, sternly they stood

Of all their mischief, the king was aware!

Getting lectured in that time was surely no good!

"O' King, it was Angada" Hanuman declared

"To take us to Madhuvan, he was the one,

At first, to agree, we all were scared

But Angada told us, that it would be fun

The crowned prince, we could never deny

Thus to Madhuvan, did we all then go

We couldn't disagree with the nephew thy

To prince Angada, we couldn't say no"

Before Angada had a chance to protest

With Hanuman did everyone else agree

Angada's voice was shadowed by the rest

Everyone gladly ignored Angada's plea

Laughing heartily did the king then say

"O' Hanuman, for this deed, you have done

You had all the right to enjoy your way

No one would have stopped you, to have such fun

As for Madhuvan, I will get it rebuilt

For Dadhimukha, I shall build it anew

Hence O' Hanuman, have no guilt

And right now, I have a work for you

To Sri Rama, you now go and say

About Devi Sita, he will be glad to know

This news is sure to brighten his day

To tell him of her, right now you go

Hanuman was so excited to go and tell this

To where Sri Rama was, he instantly flew

To tell him, not a word, Hanuman could miss

He wished to recite the whole story through

To Rama, he wanted to tell about everything

"O' Prabhu, Ma Sita, I have spoken to

She is there in Lanka, where Ravana is the king

Without you there, Janani is very blue

Ma Sita, is very sad for not being with thee

But to help the others, she resolved to stay

Instead she gave her Chintamani to me"

Giving it to Rama, everything else did he say

From Hanuman, the Chintamani Rama got
In it, Sita's smiling face he could see
His Sita's gentle touch on it he could spot
He realized, from him, so far was she

Rama thought about Sita's graceful smile
Onto his face, a tear found its way
The distance between them was so many a mile
He couldn't bear that she was so far away

For him, Hanuman had crossed the Sea,
And so many troubles he had to slip through
Just so that, his Sita he could see
And pull Rama out of this blue

To Hanuman did Rama then go and embrace
And then said, "O' Hanuman, thank you
For me, you travelled to so far a place
For me, over the mighty ocean, you flew

I can only thank you, with my heart all
More than this, I have nothing to give thee
For what you have done, anything I give is small
Thank you, O' Hanuman, for doing this for me"

From Hanuman came tears of delight
Sri Rama, himself had blessed him
In his heart, he could feel devotion bright
And this devotion could never get dim

Rama looked at him, like a father at his son
Hanuman did not need anything more than this
Happier than Hanuman right now, were none
Sri Rama's name itself was Hanuman's bliss

Sugriva by then reached Rama's side
He told him, "O' Rama, I am very glad for thee
For this, anything you need, I shall provide
I shall do anything to set Devi Sita free"

Rama thanked Sugriva for the words of his
About Lanka, they asked Hanuman to recount
Not a single detail did Hanuman miss
For every bit of Lanka, did he account

Hanuman told them all about it
Of Lanka he told them all about
Of Lanka he described every bit
Lanka he described inside out

Where Sita was, now that they know
They all could not stay there anymore
Thus they all decided to go
To head down to the south shore

Jambavan called for his army of bears
And Sugriva's subjects were called for aid
The soldiers' zeal was oil on the flares
Out of them, the strongest army was made

Meanwhile in Lanka, in Ravana's hall
On his lavish throne did Ravana sit
He was accompanied by his subjects all
Lanka was still recovering from Hanuman's hit

Vibhishana in the hall, stood up and said
"O' Brother, what you are doing is a sin
There shall be a deadly war coming ahead
And in it, there is no way we can win

To burn Lanka, only one was enough
Imagine what their army can do
Beating them will be very tough
To win, our chances are very few"

"What do you mean?" Ravana replied
"You wanted me to fear that Rama and run
Vibhishana, you are on whose side
To doubt my powers, you are the only one

That Rama wants Sita back
So you are telling me to do so?
Vibhishana, my bravery, you surely lack
Like you, I cannot stoop so low!"

"O' Brother, but you are not right,
For the actions you have done are wrong
They surely don't display your might
For doing these, you cannot claim to be strong

O' Brother, I am telling this for you
Against Sri Rama, you cannot survive
No matter how you dodge it, this is true
If you go against him, you cannot stay alive -"

"Vibhishana! That's the end of my limit!
Because you are my kin I have tolerated thee
By praising him, you are digging your own pit
What nerve do you have, to belittle me!

You are banished from Lanka, right now!
Don't ever come back to show me your face
For Lanka is no longer the house of thou
Of you, in Lanka, I should never find a trace"

Vibhishana then left, with one place in mind,
He left to reach the other shore
There Sri Rama, did he hope to find
For he was not Ravana's ally anymore

Meanwhile Rama and others came to the beach
They now started planning what to do
The other side, they all had to reach
But how do they cross the whole ocean through

"These many people," Sugriva then said,
"We cannot easily take them across the sea
But leaving them here, we cannot move ahead
For O' Rama, they have to fight along with thee

For them, we cannot build so many a boat

And we also require the wood that strong

A bridge is too hard to keep afloat

And to build it, takes a time too long"

Held up in this tangle were they all

None of them were able to find a way

Themselves out of this problem, they couldn't haul

They were thinking about this all through the day

Vibhishana just then reached the shore

He heard of what they were talking about

Since he is not under Ravana anymore

He can side with Rama without a doubt

Soon to Sri Rama did he then go

But Sugriva stopped him then and there

"O' Rama", he said, "This man is our foe,

For he is Ravana's brother, hence beware"

Hanuman replied, "A foe to us, he may not be,

For he seemed to know about virtue and sin

He also wishes for Ma Sita to be free

Thus, to us, he seems to be a kin"

"O' Hanuman" Vibhishana then replied

"What you have spoken is true

I came all the way here to your side

With the sole intention to help you

Time and again, I warned brother mine

I told him what he was doing is vice

I told Ravana, he was being malign

I knew for this he has to pay his price

For siding with Dharma, Ravana sent me away

For that, he banished me from his land

Thus to Sri Rama, I have come all the way,

To help Devi Sita, I too, shall lend my hand"

"Fine, O' Vibhishana", Rama replied

"If Hanuman trusts you, so do I

From today on, you are on our side

You are hence, a part of us hereby"

"Thank you, O' Rama" Vibhishana said

"But while coming, your problem I got to know

We need to cross the sea to move ahead

But with these many people, it is hard to go

To this O' Rama, I know a way

In order to get us across the Sea,

To the sea god, Samudra, you have to pray

For he is the only one who can help thee"

Listening to him, Rama prayed to the ocean

He prayed and prayed for days through

He prayed and prayed with utmost devotion

Yet the Sea God Samudra did not come into view

For a long while did they await

Rama's limits did this seem to test

A moment longer now he couldn't wait

A moment longer now he couldn't rest

From his prayer then did Rama stand

From the quiver, one arrow, he then took

And placed it, on the bow in his hand

Then towards the ocean did he look

The arrow, he aimed it towards the ocean

He held the arrow, ready to set free

But just before the arrow was set in motion

There appeared, Samudra, the God of Sea

"O' Rama!" came the Sea God's reply

"For the animals in me, spare my life

For they all shall be dead, if I die

Instead, I shall help you in saving your wife

The laws of physics I cannot negate

Thus I cannot split the sea for you

Thus a bridge on me, you shall create

For this, all the living shall help you through

If you write your name on any stone

In water, it shall never sink

A bridge you build with those alone

The two lands like this, you can link

Nala is the great Vishvakarma's son

He is one of the allies of thou

By him the planning shall be done

To build the bridge, he has the know-how"

Saying so did the Sea God leave

But the arrow in Rama's hand stay put

An arrow once put, he does not retrieve

Thus he aimed it at a mountain's foot

In a flash did the mountain then fall,

In a second, collapsed its peak

In it were killed the monsters all

In agony did all those demons shriek

"Let us build the bridge" did Rama then say

The work began the moment he spoke

Hanuman shattered a hill, near the bay

The bridge was built with the hill that broke

Rama's name was etched on every stone

On water did they stay afloat

But in this task they were not alone

For Ramakaarya every creature was devote

Once Rama noticed a squirrel small

It rolled itself in the beach sand

Then into the sea did it quickly crawl

And ran back again, onto the land

Then the tiny squirrel did Rama ask,
"What are you doing? O' Small one,
You seem to be doing some unique task
As into the ocean you seem to run"

The squirrel then said in its sweet tone
"O' Rama, to lift the rocks I am too small
With these tiny hands, I cannot lift a stone
Thus I couldn't help you, like the others all

So, this sand, I started carrying to the sea
To fill in the gap between the blocks,
This is the only way, I can help thee
Since I cannot carry those mighty rocks"

Rama was dazzled by the squirrel's devotion
Even such a small creature wanted to aid
The zeal in its eyes was larger than the ocean
Such devotion could never be repaid

The squirrel onto his palm Rama took

And with his hand, patted its face

So blessed did the squirrel look

As Rama's warm hand, caressed with grace

The mighty bridge was built anon

On it, Lanka did Rama plan to reach

On that mighty bridge they walked upon

They finally came to Lanka's beach

"I wish to avoid war" Rama then said

"I do not wish innocents to be hurt

I do not want any of you dead

Any bloodshed, I seek to avert

Angada; convincing are the words of thee

Go to Ravana and tell him there

Tell him to send my Sita to me

Only then his life I shall spare"

As per Rama's word, Angada went
As a messenger he entered Ravana's hall
And spoke, "On Sri Rama's order I was sent,
As his messenger, I have come to you all

Ravana, what you did is a terrible crime
Thus, to Sri Rama, send Ma Sita back
If not, a war shall strike in short time
And you will never survive our attack"

With anger then did Ravana then roar,
"How brave of you to come warn me,
Not having a bit of fear you walk through my door
And expect me to shiver at thee?!

Sita will never return for she is mine,
And for coming here, you shall be dead
By talking to me you crossed your line
Soon you shall regret whatever you said"

"Ha!" At Ravana did Angada sneer
"You really think you can kill me?
Right now I challenge everyone here
To try and lift my right foot free"

Angada stomped his foot on the floor
And motioned them all to charge
Towards his foot they ran with a roar
They struck Angada's foot at large

But whatever they did, his foot did not shift
Yet to move his foot they tried and tried
His foot, no matter what, they could not lift
Soon the courtiers' will power dried

Ravana, himself, then finally came
To lift Angada's foot he bent low
With anger, his insides were aflame
Yet to Angada, his power, he had to show

Angada stopped the king and then said
"Ravana, do not touch my feet,
Touch Sri Rama's if seek not to be dead
If not, your end you shall soon meet"

Ravana's anger now burst from inside
Clenching his fist, he could not stand still
Angada had just stabbed his pride
Instantly he ordered his men to kill

Angada did they all try to chase
But, for them he was way too fast
Angada swiftly left that place
And left all of them aghast

To Rama, he went and told all he had done,
He told him of what Ravana said
The preparations for war had soon begun
A war was to happen shortly ahead

Meanwhile to Sita did Ravana then go

A magician named Vidyujjihva went with him

With magic he made Rama's head and bow

Ravana was sure this would make Sita grim

He hoped that if he showed Rama's end

Then Sita would weaken and stay

The rest of her life, here she will spend

She would remain with Ravana everyday

He walked up to Sita and then spoke

"Sita, Rama and his men are dead

And to prove that this is not a joke

I brought you his bow and head"

The head in his hand, Sita saw

To her senses did she barely cling

Out of her, she felt her soul withdraw

It was surely her Rama, her everything

In front of Ravana, Sita stood still

Her shock did her eyes openly display

Yet a single tear Sita did not spill

She withheld, in her, all signs of dismay

It was like her life had been sucked out

And all that remained was her empty shell

In agony did her heart scream and shout

Without Rama, the world had turned to hell

Sita felt it was the end of her life

Yet she did not show it through her eye

Because, still she was her Rama's wife

Thus in front of Ravana she could not cry

Without Rama, she was incomplete

The world had collapsed all around

Then slowly all her power left her feet

And she fell unconscious on to the ground

To Ravana, just then a minister came
To ask him for the battle scheme
Ravana then left to discuss the same
To discuss the same with his tactics team

Ravana left, leaving Sita there
Trijata then came to Sita's aid
Sita soon woke up, in deep despair
All her glow just seemed to fade

To Sita, the truth did Trijata tell
"O' Sita, what Ravana showed is not true
Of Vidyujjihva it was merely a spell
It was a petty ploy to deceive you"

Sita was relieved by what Trijata told
Her Rama was well and fine
Her breath, she finally had controlled
And to her face returned her shine

The battle soon began the next day
Ravana thought of the Vanaras too low
Them, he thought, his men could easily slay
There Ravana deeply underestimated his foe

He carelessly sent his troops ahead
But for them the Vanaras were too strong
Soon many of his soldiers were dead
The Vanaras were leading after not so long

Then came Indrajit, Ravana's eldest son,
He was a warrior of extreme skill
He started defeating the Vanaras one by one
So many of the Vanaras did he kill

The two armies were equal by sunset
On both sides many men had died
Ravana finally realized that Rama was a threat
A more rigid plan did he then decide

The injured were tended during the night,

During the same time were cremated the dead

They were thanked for their brave fight

They were thanked for the blood that they had shed

Rama cremated even the men of his foe

But Sugriva did not understand why

That for their nemesis, why stoop so low

Why for their enemies' men, they had to cry

Rama did Sugriva then finally ask,

"O' Rama, for those men why did you pray?

Why did you do this unneeded task?

When you could have just let their bodies decay"

To Sugriva then did Rama reply,

"O' Sugriva, they were our foes that is true

But they are our foes only until they die

And after death, I must respect them too

Sugriva, we have enemies as long as we be

But after death, they do not remain so

From the bond of hatred they are set free

Thus respect to them we must show"

"O Rama, what you have said is right

We only have foes until our last breath

Only when living, do we all fight

There are enemies none, beyond death"

Ravana was a little alert the next day

He thought of his plan through and through

In hope that they would be leading today

Being wary he sent his ministers few

But into the battle did Lakshmana come

Most of the ministers did he defeat

In his hands, did many succumb

Single handedly he performed such a feat

The battle soon did the Vanaras lead
Indrajit then came onto the battle field
He charged at them, with great speed
The losses of his army he soon healed

Rama and Lakshmana did he then attack
The Nagastra on them did he use
Both the brothers then fell aback
Deadly snakes did the Nagastra produce

Both the brothers, the snakes had wound
Them did the snakes then entangle
This made them fall to the ground
Them the serpents then started to strangle

Both of them struggled to be free
Yet the robust snakes they couldn't move
A mighty eagle did they then see
With ease the snakes did he remove

High above did the eagle soar

In the blue sky did he glide

The brothers were not choked anymore

All the Nagastra's powers had died

As the Vahana of Vishnu he was renowned

Garuda was this eagle's name,

When he knew that by snakes, Rama was bound

To help Sri Rama, he swiftly came

As soon as he did what he could do

Garuda then left and flew away

Back to the battle were the brothers two

But the battle soon ended for the day

The next day the battle began anew

The army that day, Indrajit led

With powerful weapons he roared through

Because of him many Vanaras were dead

Ravana also sent his other son

Him did Angada then beat

In their fight, Angada had won

Him did Angada easily defeat

Indrajit then, did Lakshmana strike

A fierce battle did they both fight

Both their strengths were almost alike

Both of them had enormous might

They both fought all day long

Yet their fight did not seem to slow

Lakshmana was extremely strong

But to him, Indrajit gave the toughest blow

The battle Lakshmana seemed to lead

Thus a poisoned arrow Indrajit shot

Due to its wound did Lakshmana bleed

He then fell to the ground on the spot

Soon after the sky grew dim

Indrajit left Lakshmana lying there

The arrow's poison still piercing him

Lakshmana was rushed to the Vanaras' care

Medicinal herbs did they then apply

The arrow from him, did they procure

But to the poison, no matter how they try

The doctors there could not find a cure

Then did Hanuman swiftly go

And a doctor called Sushena he brought

To him, Lakshmana, did they show

He then examined the area where he was shot

To Rama then did Sushena say

"O Rama, the wound is very grim

To save him there is only one way

But his odds of surviving are very slim

The herb Sanjivani is very rare

Only in the mighty Himalayas is it found

A medicine with that we must prepare

And around his slash it needs to be wound"

Rama was destroyed by the words he spoke

He could barely stop his tears welling within

Thinking of Lakshmana, his heart broke

His heart ached with grief for his dearest kin

Onto his knees then Rama fell

He stayed kneeling on top of the floor

In his eyes tears started to dwell

He could no longer bear this pain anymore

"My Sita, my life was taken from me

Because of him, I was able to bear that pain

Without him by my side, what would I be?

If he is gone, for me, what would remain?"

Hanuman couldn't see Rama so low
Hence to Rama, then did Hanuman reply
"O' Prabhu, to the Himalayas I shall go
Till those mighty mountains I shall fly

The Sanjivani herb I will surely get
I can even fly till the Sun for you
But O' Prabhu, I cannot see your eyes wet
Thus, O' Prabhu, do not feel so blue"

A flicker of hope to Rama he gave
Taking his blessings, Hanuman took flight
Lakshmana surely, he has to save
To Himalayas, he headed with all his might

Hanuman leaving, a spy had seen
To Ravana he told all about it
To Ravana he narrated the entire scene
He explained everything, bit by bit

Of Lakshmana's strength Ravana was aware

Hanuman going to Himalayas he had to prevent

Thus to prevent him from going there

The demon Kalanemi, Ravana sent

Kalanemi then went, and in Hanuman's way

A graceful Ashram did he then create

In the form of a sage, there did he stay

And for Hanuman to arrive did he wait

Soon to the Ashram did Hanuman come

He had come to drink some water there

From the disguised demon he took water from

But about Kalanemi he was unaware

After he thanked the sage, the sage then said

"O' Hanuman, my blessings are with you

If you seek victory against the army Ravana led

This holy lake's water, take a dip into"

To the sage's words did Hanuman agree

Into the waters did he then go

And as he bent up to his knee

He noticed a crocodile in the water below

Trying to bite him, the beast flung its head

But Hanuman punched it before it could

The crocodile then seemed to be dead

But it became an Apsara who gracefully stood

She then said, "O' Hanuman, thank you,

The curse that I had, did you destroy

You have saved me from such a blue

And into my life you brought back the joy

Thus, I must help you, as a way to repay

O' Hanuman, a demon has morphed into a sage

For killing you, he was waiting all day

For trapping you he has set this stage"

About Kalanemi, Hanuman got to know,

The Apsara did he then thank,

Within seconds he defeated his foe

In moments, Kalanemi laid there, blank

After defeating him, Hanuman left that place

The Himalayas did he soon reach

They were covered in white, filled with grace

At their beauty and might, Hanuman lost his speech

The mountain Dronagiri then came into sight

He got onto it, and began his quest

He searched for the herb with all his might

He searched the north, south, east and west

"There are so many herbs over here

Which one is which, how will I know?

All look the same, nothing is clear

Empty handed, to Sri Rama, I cannot go

Sushena, with me, I should've brought

I just came flying here with feverish haste

But unlike me, he knows what is what!

Then, this time wouldn't have gone to waste

I should've, at least, asked him to describe it

I just came flying here, with such a speed

I have made a mistake, I must admit

But complaining won't get me what I need

Now the easiest task, let me do

Let me take the whole mountain there

Let Sushena search the mountain through

Of searching for the herb let him take care"

Hanuman prayed to Rama in his mind,

And to a huge size did he then grow

In height the mountains he left behind

At his slightest breath did the wind blow

Hanuman's presence did the animals sense
In the havoc and fear, they ran away
Birds flew away from the forest dense
And out of the mountain did the animals stray

Dronagiri with a single hand did Hanuman lift
He then took a jump, into the air
And towards Lanka did he swiftly drift
While carrying the mountain in his hands bare

Without a break Hanuman briskly went on
While carrying Dronagiri in his hand
He reached Lanka before the break of dawn
Finally in Lanka did Hanuman land

He dropped the hill with a loud thud
Soon flew away the creatures around
Onto the floor did the melted snow flood
And all the soldiers did Hanuman astound

Sushena said, "Anjaneya, what did you do?!
I told you to get an herb so small
But with that mighty hill, till here you flew
Is getting the herb so hard after all?"

"O' Sushena", then did Hanuman reply
"Which herb was which, it wasn't clear
Since I did not possess the wisdom thy
Thus, I brought the mountain itself here"

Sushena then said with a smile
"O' Hanuman, you have done an impossible deed
You came here, carrying that, all the while
O' Hanuman, you are the best indeed!"

Soon Lakshmana did Sushena cure
Finally Sri Rama felt his heart
From so far, the herbs did Hanuman procure
Their bond had become a thing, none could part

Embracing Hanuman, Rama then told
"O' Hanuman, with all my heart, I thank you
You have done deeds unheard and untold
Right now, there is nothing you cannot do

For all the tasks that you have done
I don't know how to thank thee
Hanuman, to me you are a son
You are always a son to Sita and me"

With joy, did Hanuman's face glow
Hanuman replied, with tears of bliss
"O' Prabhu, in what this world could ever bestow
Nothing could ever mean more than this"

Hanuman then bent on to his knee
And with devotion, touched Rama's feet
"O' Prabhu, chanting your name is a boon to me
And with these words, that boon is complete"

Of Kalanemi's death did Ravana hear

About winning he seemed to worry a bit

They were stronger than they seemed to appear

For the next step he was at the end of his wit

Of his people Ravana then thought

Who could turn the battle in a day?

The answer to that Ravana finally got

To victory this was their only way

"Wake him up!" did he then scream

The people were startled by his resolve

How to wake up Kumbhakarna from his dream?

But this was a problem they had to solve

A younger brother was Kumbhakarna to the king

For months and months he had been asleep

He had been asleep not doing a thing

They had to wake him up from that dream deep

Kumbhakarna was a man made of stone

He was a man as huge as a hill

He was one of the most powerful men ever known

He was a soldier of extreme skill

Now in a futile try to make him rise

Him, with a hundred elephants did they hit

But compared to him, they were like flies

Kumbhakarna did not move a bit

Big big drums did they then beat

The beats diced his ears like a dagger's blade

Yet his deep doze they did not defeat

Dissipated were the deeds the soldiers made

Then arrows at him did they shoot

To him, they were like needles thin

They then straight away, used force brute

Yet over Kumbhakarna's sleep they failed to win

After thousands of tries, was he finally awake
Straight to Ravana did he then go
"O' Brother, my sleep why did you break?
The reason for this I seek to know"

Pleased to see him, Ravana replied,
"Kumbhakarna! It is good to see you
I want you to fight a war by my side
Our losses in the war, you can undo"

Of all that happened Ravana told
Kumbhakarna was enraged by the king
His anger inside, he could no longer hold
How could his brother do such a thing!

"O' Brother, what have you done?
Lady Sita is Sri Rama's wife!
For your pride a war you have begun
You made the gravest sin of your life

You also sent Vibhishana away,

What our brother said was very much right

Good people I do not seek to slay,

Thus, for you, I shall not fight"

"O' Kumbhakarna, I do not need you to lecture me

Vibhishana has already done that for you

Now, I can win only with the power of thee

Now fight for me like a brother true!

You know I cannot turn back now

Not after so many of my men are dead

Thus lend me the power of thou

And give them the death that they all dread!"

Unwillingly so, Kumbhakarna agreed

The next day, he entered the ground

He attacked his foes with mighty speed

He soon spread havoc all around

He was challenged by Hanuman then and there,

They both fought with almost equal might

The battle was almost set in flare

So fiercely did both of them fight

To that place then Lakshmana came

"O' Kumbhakarna, I challenge thee

You are a soldier as strong as your fame

If so, then come and fight me!"

Then to him did Kumbhakarna reply,

"A soldier's strength is that of his strongest foe,

O' Lakshmana, I seek to fight the brother thy

For Rama here, is the strongest I know"

"Then if that is the case", Rama then said

"O' Kumbhakarna, you are a soldier true

I shall fight thee until one of us is dead

O' Kumbhakarna, it is an honor to fight you"

Rama then began his fight,

He then lifted his mighty bow

To the enemies it was a fearful sight

As he plucked the string to release the arrow

The sound itself made the enemies dread

It, itself felt like a lightning flashed

Rather than fighting, they all hoped to be dead

Whenever he fought, the enemy's hopes were crashed

But as soon as he enters the battle place

For his men, he is the courage and hope

As soon as they see his graceful face

With any enemy, they now can cope

Equally did they both fight

But soon did Rama seem to lead

Kumbhakarna acknowledged Rama's might

He spoke, "O' Rama, you are the strongest indeed!"

At that moment Rama sliced his head
"O' Kumbhakarna, it was an honor to fight you"
The mighty Kumbhakarna was finally dead
Into the streets his sliced head then flew

His mighty body then fell aback
On to the floor did it then propel
Its own people did it seem to attack
As onto Ravana's soldiers the body fell

Rama then went to Vibhishana and told,
"O' Vibhishana, I am sorry for what I have done
Your brother was a man, true and bold
He was a mighty soldier, second to none"

Then to Rama did Vibhishana reply
"O' Rama, to apologize, there is no need
I was prepared, the moment I sought refuge thy
That for Dharma, this was a necessary deed"

Of his brother's death Ravana got to know,

His hopes were almost crushed with this

Till now he thought of Rama so low

And realizing Rama's strength, he seemed to miss

He then called for Indrajit and said,

"The Nikumbhila Yagna you start right now

With that the enemies are sure to be dead

With that no one can defeat me and thou"

To conduct the Yagna did they plan

With this their path to victory was clear

Under Indrajit the Yagna soon began

Slowly, Rama's men started to disappear

Sugriva noticed the army's number sink

He thus went and asked Nala about it

Both did not know why the army began to shrink

It was slowly becoming smaller, bit by bit

To them Vibhishana then came and spoke,
"The result of their Yagna this must've been
The Goddess Nikumbhila they are trying to invoke
If they succeed, in this war, we can never win

Like this everyone will begin to fade,
From here on, our people will only decrease
Like this, slowly, everyone will be preyed
To prevent this, that Yagna must cease"

Lakshmana then came and said,
"The Yagna's obstruction you will surely see
I won't stop until Indrajit is dead
Hence, O' Vibhishana, leave this to me"

Early, the next day did he go
Along with him, even Hanuman went
They both went to stop their foe
The Yagna at all costs they must prevent

Inside a cave did Indrajit pray
Lakshmana and all then went in there
Soon of arrows there was an array
The Yagna was soon set in flare

The men who were lost began to come back
This meant that the Yagna did stall
Enraged, with his army, did Indrajit attack
With his army, he attacked them all

Indrajit challenged Lakshmana on that ground
To their speed, the eyes couldn't follow along
They caused destruction all around
Once again they were almost equally strong

But Lakshmana soon seemed to lead the fight
Thus into the clouds did Indrajit then go
And shot arrows at him while out of sight
Thus Lakshmana couldn't attack from below

Then Hanuman, Lakshmana got onto
Hanuman then flew, deep into the sky
Towards Indrajit, Hanuman then flew
Carrying Lakshmana, till there, did he fly

They both fought hard even in the air
But finally Lakshmana sliced Indrajit's head
His body fell onto the ground from there
At last even Indrajit also was dead

Indrajit's death reached the king's ear,
With this his blood was set on fire
Now for his victory only one path is clear
He, himself must destroy that army entire

"Ha! What is that Rama to me", he sneered
"To them he might be strong, but not for me,
For I am the most powerful and feared
Hence how he shall run, I will go and see!"

He entered the battlefield the next day
Hanuman was the first to challenge him
A catastrophe, or such was their frey
They both fought a battle grim

Ravana was astounded by Hanuman's might
To Hanuman he then spoke in praise
"Till date you gave me, the toughest fight
Even me, did your strength amaze"

The battleground Rama then came to
To Ravana he then came and said,
"O' Ravana, as this army's head, I challenge you
And as Sita's husband, I shall see you dead"

Soon did their brutal battle begin,
They both fought with humongous might
It was impossible to say who would win
Even the nature was scared of their fight

Their battle began to quiver the land
The skies started to roar in ire
The rocks around had turned to sand
The whole ground was set in fire

But soon the upper hand did Rama get
Ravana he was about to defeat
But by then the Sun had begun to set
Thus his weapon did Rama retreat

He then spoke to Ravana standing there
"I realized this is not your real might
Till tomorrow I am giving you time to prepare
Then, for real, come to me and fight"

With those words, Ravana couldn't stand still
But he cannot attack after the night fall
Rama, then and there, he wanted to kill
But for now this battle had to stall

With his strongest weapons he came the next day

With anger his insides were still aflame

The price for what he said, Rama must pay

Thus he challenged Rama as soon as he came

Using his powers, into a giant he grew

As tall as a mountain did he then grow

Hence on top of Hanuman, Rama flew

With Hanuman, to that height Rama could go

They fought like that for a time so long

It was a battle never before seen

Both of them were extremely strong

The most powerful men this was a battle between

Lord Indra then came to Rama and said,

"O' Rama, the other men Hanuman must defeat

Therefore you use my chariot instead

This way the enemy's power, you can deplete"

Onto that chariot Rama then got

Ravana, he began to strike anew

Then towards Ravana's head an arrow he shot

Which sliced his head and body into two

Ravana let out a screeching cry

Finally Ravana seemed to meet his end

At last Ravana seemed certain to die

But out of his neck did another head extend

Rama was surprised at what he had seen

He had never seen anything like this before

Again he sliced Ravana's head clean

But another head protruded once more

No matter how many times Rama cut his head

Another head seemed to come out of it

No matter what, Ravana was not dead

No matter how many times his neck was slit

To a perplexed Rama, Vibhishana then told
"O' Rama, to kill Ravana, there is only one way
All his powers near his stomach does he hold
Thus that part of him you must slay"

Rama listened to what Vibhishana spoke
The Brahmastra did he then procure
As taught by Sage Agastya, Sun God, did he invoke
With this he had to succeed for sure

The Brahmastra towards Ravana, he then shot
Ravana did it then brutally hit
Ravana then fell to the ground on the spot
At last Ravana was defeated by it

To Ravana then did Vibhishana come,
"O' Brother, now see where you are
For your own sins did you succumb?
To Lanka, your crimes have now left a scar

If only you had let Devi Sita go
I wouldn't have to see you like this
You would never have had to stoop so low
We could have all lived together in bliss

O' Brother, what sin did I commit?
That I must witness the death thy"
Even though he was prepared for it
Vibhishana couldn't see his brother die

Ravana at last realized his crime
"O' Vibhishana, at least now you forgive me
I cannot stop the passage of time
But at least one last time, I have seen thee

O' Vibhishana, you were always right
It was foolish of me not to listen to you
Then I could have avoided this fight
Then these times we wouldn't have gone through"

He saw Rama and Hanuman on the verge of his death
Finally realizing who they are
Smiling Ravana took his final breath
Feeling his soul drift afar

No matter what, he was a king, great and true
He always stood on the choices he made
His last rites did Vibhishana then do
To him, his respects, Rama also paid

Rama then declared Vibhishana as the king
He asked Hanuman to tell Sita that they won
"Such a joy to Janani it would bring"
Thinking of that, till there did he run

To Sita did Hanuman soon go and say
As soon as she heard that, her face was aglow
Vibhishana escorted her through the way
To where Rama was, did she then go

As she saw her Rama, standing there
"Rama! Aryaputra!" did she excitedly exclaim
Of where she was she wasn't even aware
As towards Rama she delightedly came

"Stay there!" Rama suddenly said
"Do not come any closer to me,
As a Kshatriya, Ravana, did I behead
It was only my duty to set you free

In another house you stayed for a year
Your purity, you now cannot prove
Therefore, to me, do not come near
Towards me, do not make a move"

With disbelief, Sita looked at him
He was desperately trying to avoid her eye
To Sita, the world suddenly turned grim
She looked at him for answers, not knowing why

With his words, the world did Rama astound
They never thought, such a thing, Rama would do
Shocked with this, was the world around
They couldn't imagine what Sita was going through

Hanuman was angry at Rama for the first time
"What is Prabhu doing?" he then thought
"For such punishment, what is Janani's crime?
What deeds of her brought such distraught"

Before he realized, tears slowly fell
But he couldn't wipe them off right now,
"About Janani, to Prabhu, I was the one to tell
I feel like this is my fault somehow"

For the first time, with Rama did he disagree
But against Rama he could never go
"I cannot oppose him, he is a father to me
Yet I cannot see my mother Sita so low"

At Rama did Lakshmana continue to stare

With anger his eyes were going red

With anger his insides were at flare

Yet clenching his fists he stood silently instead

"My brother's word as Dharma did I believe

If so, what kind of Dharma this is?

By following Dharma what did I achieve?

If it meant seeing Ma Sita like this"

He opened his lips, in an attempt to say something

Yet out of them, no words have come

To go against Rama, himself, he couldn't bring

Yet with anger his insides were going numb

Finally Sita was the one to speak,

"O' Rama, what sins did I commit

That from me such penance you seek?

That for such punishment, you see me fit

O' Rama, are these words truly by you?

I have heard the words you have spoken

Are these the words of a Kshatriya true?

Because of thy words, my heart is broken

O' Rama, is this you talking to me?

These are not the words of the Rama I know

I never thought they could be said by thee

Now I only have one way to go"

Still looking at Rama, did she then say,

"Right here, right now, I shall jump into fire

For me, O' Rama, this is the only way

O' Lakshmana, for me, prepare a pyre!"

Lakshmana turned to Sita, his eyes wide

He so wished, he could save her from that blue

Even to spill out, his tears had dried

But he had to do what she told him to do

To seek permission, Rama did he see
Of emotion his face seemed to be void
He did not say yes, yet he didn't disagree
While Sita's eyes, he still seemed to avoid

Lakshmana soon prepared a pyre there,
Fire in it did he then light
Sita then jumped into that flare
Seemingly eaten by the fire's might

In sorrow was the whole world around
That happening, they all couldn't prevent
Ashamed, they all looked to the ground
By no means for this, can they repent

While the world was dwelling in shame
Rama looked into the flames afar
With Sita, the Fire God himself came
On Sita, there wasn't even a scar

Addressing Rama, did the Fire God say

"O' Rama, there is no sin that Sita has done

There is no need for you to keep her away

In this world, purer than her are none"

Rama smiled and to Sita he said,

"O' Sita, I am sorry, forgive me

You, into such glum, I have led

But I did not want the world to judge thee

Who you are, I always knew,

But that, the world needed to know,

I cannot bear someone judging you

Thus who you are, to them, I had to show

I couldn't bear to have you away

I couldn't bear that your heart I broke

I couldn't bear to see you that way

I couldn't bear the way I spoke

The flowers lose their fragrance without you

Without you, the rivers cease to flow

Without you, the world loses its hue

Without you, Sita, the Sun loses its glow

I am complete only with you by my side

O' Sita, I am incomplete without thee

In my heart do you always reside

O' Sita, I hope you forgive me"

At Rama, did Sita then smile and reply

"O' Rama, you do not need to ask me this

Forever I shall always stay by the side thy

For you are the only reason for my bliss"

Finally each other did they embrace

Lakshmana and Hanuman rejoiced in delight

The universe was once again was filled with grace

The world, once again, was shining bright

By Indra's boon came back the soldiers lost

All of Sugriva's men came back alive

Thus in this war their life wasn't the cost

Did all of Sugriva's soldiers survive

Vibhishana's crowning was done with a roar

To leave for Ayodhya did they then prepare

Meanwhile, that hill did Hanuman restore

To Himalayas he went, and kept it there

After he came back, to Ayodhya did they leave

On the Pushpaka Vimana did they all ride

How many ever people that flight can receive

And always for one more person it has space beside

Bharata came to receive them at the gate

His face brightened as he saw his brother

For fourteen years it was so hard to wait

Finally the four brothers embraced each other

Rama, finally Bharata got to meet

To him, did Bharata and Shatrughna pray

Bharata returned the sandals to Rama's feet

Delighted to see their brother, were they

The joy back to Ayodhya did Rama bring

For Sita and Rama, it was a festival there

They celebrated the coming of their queen and king

And for Rama's crowning did they prepare

They celebrated it through day and night

Even the night shone like day

Wherever you go, there was light

Such joy did the people display

Crowning of Sita and Rama was done with joy,

It was done with extreme pomp and show

Their coronation did the whole world enjoy

In that joy did the whole city glow

Rama gave presents to all who had come

The one Hanuman got was the best of all

By Sita's hands he received it from

Of pearls it was a necklace small

Hanuman examined it through and through

He then plucked out a pearl from it

And that pearl, behind he threw

Like that he threw it all, bit by bit

Astounded, did Sita then say,

"O' Hanuman, with love that was given to thee

Yet why did you throw it away?

That was gifted to you by Rama and me"

"O' Janani, it was given by you and Prabhu you said,

But in it, you both I could not find

Neither in the pearls nor in the thread

Thus I threw that necklace behind"

Then did Vibhishana intervene

"O' Hanuman, then if that is true,

Them both, in you, have you seen

Are Sita and Rama there in you?"

"Oh yes, they both do reside in me

In my heart both Prabhu and Janani are there

I can show it to you if you wish to see"

Saying so he slit his chest without a care

His own chest did Hanuman then slit

His own chest he then sliced apart

Both Sita and Rama were there in it

They both were truly there in his heart

Due to Lord Brahma's boon did it soon heal

Within seconds the slash had healed clean

Hanuman's love for them both did it reveal

Sita was astounded by what she had seen

Hanuman gave Sita extreme bliss
Her radiance was clearly seen in her face
Rama who was seeing all of this
To Hanuman did he come and embrace

The city of Ayodhya was aglow
The whole city rejoiced that day
Celebrations were done with pomp and show
Such joy and hue did Kosala display

There was music and dance everywhere
They were happier than they could ever be
Their king and queen with them were there
To the eyes it was a pleasure to see

Rama was the greatest king Ayodhya knew
In ruling Ayodhya did they succeed
The kingdom never again lost its hue
Like that Kosala, did Sita and Rama lead

Here, sitting below the same tree

I turn the last page of this book

The tale of Sita and Rama did I just see

This epic Ramayana still gets me in a hook

– Veda Samhita

"Started Writing - October 2019

Finished writing - 22nd August 2021

First Published (Self published) - 12th March 2022"